SOARING THROUGH THE BIBLE

SKIP HEITZIG

HARVEST HOUSE PUBLISHERS
EUGENE, OREGON

Unless otherwise indicated, all Scripture quotations are taken from the Holy Bible, New Living Translation, copyright © 1996, 2004, 2015 by Tyndale House Foundation. Used by permission of Tyndale House Publishers, Inc., Carol Stream, Illinois 60188. All rights reserved.

Verses marked TLB are taken from The Living Bible, copyright © 1971. Used by permission of Tyndale House Publishers, Inc., Carol Stream, Illinois 60188. All rights reserved.

Verses marked NKJV are taken from the New King James Version®. Copyright © 1982 by Thomas Nelson, Inc. Used by permission. All rights reserved.

Cover design and Illustration by Darren Welch Design

Interior Illustrations by Joshua Taylor

Interior design by Chad Dougherty

Published in association with the William K. Jensen Literary Agency, 119 Bampton Court, Eugene, Oregon 97404

HARVEST KIDS is a trademark of The Hawkins Children's LLC. Harvest House Publishers, Inc., is the exclusive licensee of the trademark HARVEST KIDS.

Soaring Through the Bible
Copyright © 2019 by Skip Heitzig
Published by Harvest House Publishers
Eugene, Oregon 97408
www.harvesthousepublishers.com

ISBN 978-0-7369-7557-5 (pbk.)
ISBN 978-0-7369-7769-2 (eBook)

Library of Congress Cataloging-in-Publication Data

Names: Heitzig, Skip, author.
Title: Soaring through the Bible / Skip Heitzig.
Description: Eugene : Harvest House Publishers, 2019. | Juvenile version of author's The Bible at 30,000 feet.
Identifiers: LCCN 2019000380 (print) | LCCN 2019007303 (ebook) | ISBN 9780736977692 (ebook) | ISBN 9780736975575 (pbk.)
Subjects: LCSH: Bible—Introductions—Juvenile literature.
Classification: LCC BS539 (ebook) | LCC BS539 .H45 2019 (print) | DDC 220.6/1—dc23
LC record available at https://lccn.loc.gov/2019000380

All rights reserved. No part of this publication may be reproduced, stored in a retrieval system, or transmitted in any form or by any means—electronic, mechanical, digital, photocopy, recording, or any other—except for brief quotations in printed reviews, without the prior permission of the publisher.

Printed in the United States of America

19 20 21 22 23 24 25 26 27 / VP-CD / 10 9 8 7 6 5 4 3 2 1

CONTENTS

Get Ready for Takeoff! 5

Old Testament

Genesis 9
Exodus 15
Leviticus 21
Numbers 26
Deuteronomy 31
Joshua 36
Judges 41
Ruth 45
1 and 2 Samuel 48
1 and 2 Kings 56
1 and 2 Chronicles 63
Ezra 68
Nehemiah 72
Esther 76
Job 80
Psalms 84
Proverbs, Ecclesiastes,
   and Song of Solomon 88
Isaiah 95
Jeremiah 98
Lamentations 101

Ezekiel 104
Daniel 107
Hosea, Joel, Amos, and Obadiah 111
Jonah 117
Micah, Nahum, and Habakkuk 120
Zephaniah and Haggai 125
Zechariah and Malachi 129

New Testament

Matthew and Mark 133
Luke and John 141
Acts 149
Romans 155
1 and 2 Corinthians 160
Galatians 166
Ephesians 169
Philippians 173
Colossians 176
1 and 2 Thessalonians 178
1 and 2 Timothy 184
Titus and Philemon 189
Hebrews 193
James 197
1 and 2 Peter 200
1, 2, and 3 John and Jude 204
Revelation 210

Is Your Name in the Book? 215

GET READY FOR TAKEOFF!

Do you know how special the Bible is? It's the only book in the world that tells us who God really is and how we can know Him. There's no other book like it!

That means we need to make sure we understand what God is saying through these ancient words. Sometimes that can be hard even for me—and I've been studying the Bible for most of my life!

But I've found that a great way to understand the Bible is by an overview. Imagine flying in an airplane. The higher up you go into the air and look down, the more you can see of the earth than you can from the ground.

Now imagine if you could look at the Bible like that. You would be able to see a much bigger picture of the whole book. That's why I wrote *Soaring Through the Bible*. I want to show you a bigger picture so that you can see what the Bible is all about.

I encourage you to read *Soaring Through the Bible* from cover to cover, like a normal book. Maybe read a chapter each day. Then you'll get to know the whole story of how God made people, how people sinned against Him, and how Jesus came to save people.

Each chapter in this book has these three sections:

- *Check Your Location.* This section talks about who wrote that book of the Bible, what was happening at the time when they wrote it, and what it's about.

- *Plot Your Course.* This section gives a summary of all the action in the book: what happened and what it means.
- *Enjoy Your Trip.* This section points out some of the big ideas in each book and how you can put them into practice in your own life.

Every "Enjoy Your Trip" section includes a part called "Where's the Gospel?" Did you know every book of the Bible talks about the gospel? The gospel is the good news that God's Son, Jesus Christ, came to earth to die on the cross and save you and me from our sin. God planned the gospel from before the beginning of time—before He made the earth or even you and me! So that means the gospel pops up all throughout Scripture. The Bible will repeat certain important themes, but this is the greatest theme of all!

I want to show you that studying the Bible is fun—and even downright crazy sometimes! So as we soar through Scripture, you'll also find these special sections to enjoy:

- *Learn the Language.* The Bible wasn't originally written in English, so here you'll find what some words meant in their original language.
- *Must-See Sites.* These include interesting places and events.
- *Culture Shock.* The Bible is full of some weird and shocking things! This is where you can learn about some of them.
- *Tour Guide.* The Bible is also full of interesting people. This section gives you clues about certain people, and you have to figure out who the person is.
- *Pack Smart.* This section shows you how to not just learn about the Bible but also live out what you learn.

- *Expect the Unexpected.* This is where you'll learn some surprising facts in Scripture.

Keep a Bible near you as you read so you can look up verses when you need to and read them on your own. That way, you'll be able to remember where things are located in your Bible. Use a good translation that makes the Bible easier to understand. In this book, I used the New Living Translation (NLT) and The Living Bible (TLB). But you can use any Bible you have.

The biggest thing I want you to learn from this book is how much God loves you and how far He went to make sure you get to be with Him in heaven forever. So buckle up as we prepare to take flight and soar through the Bible!

GENESIS

Check Your Location

Moses wrote Genesis, the first book of the Bible, thousands of years ago. *Genesis* is a word that means *beginnings*. Genesis is important because it shows us that God is the Creator. It also describes the beginning of everything: life, sin, God's solution to sin, and Israel—the nation Jesus Christ would come from.

LEARN THE LANGUAGE—*Create*

In Genesis 1:1, we read that God "created" the world. The word *created* comes from a Hebrew word that means "to carve or cut out." God *carved* the world into shape like a master sculptor.

Plot Your Course

The Formation of Everything (Genesis 1–2)

The beginning of the universe is simple: God created it all. He made day and night, water and land, plants, the sun, the moon, stars, birds, bugs, sea creatures, all the animals, and His most special creation: human beings. When He was done, He called all He had made good, and then He rested.

PACK SMART

Some people wonder if God really made the world. Think about it like this: You breathe air, but can you make it? You can grow a plant, but can you make a seed? Only God can create like that. When you look closely at the world around you, it looks like it was designed. That's because it *was*. If you can believe God made the world, believing the rest of the Bible is easy.

The Fall of Humanity (Genesis 3–11)

In the Garden of Eden, God told the first people, Adam and Eve, not to eat from the tree of the knowledge of good and evil. But God also gave them free will, the ability to choose their actions. There was nothing wrong with this tree. It was just wrong to disobey God.

Satan came along in the form of a serpent, and he tempted Eve to sin—to disobey what God told her. So Eve ate some fruit from the tree, and Adam followed. This was the saddest day in the history of the human race. This is where all our problems began. Because of what Adam and Eve did—what we call *the fall*—every person sins and will die one day.

After Adam and Eve, the human race became so bad that God decided to start life over again with a huge flood. He chose the only good man He could find, Noah, to build a boat so that Noah's family and two of each animal could survive the flood of water that covered the earth.

But even after God gave people a second chance, they messed up. They built the Tower of Babel in rebellion against God. So God made everyone speak different languages. They had to stop building their rebel tower because they couldn't communicate. After that, everyone drifted apart, and God began to focus on making a special nation for Himself.

EXPECT THE UNEXPECTED

God didn't kick Adam and Eve out of the Garden of Eden because they ate that fruit. He booted them because He didn't want them to eat from the other forbidden tree—the tree of life—and be stuck in their sinful ways forever. It was actually an act of mercy!

MUST-SEE SITES—*Babel*

After the flood, God gave mankind a second chance (He loves to do that!). He told them to spread out, explore, and live awesome lives. Instead, everyone gathered together and revolted. The Tower of Babel was probably a type of pyramid built in giant steps called a *ziggurat*. By confusing everyone's language, God forced them to do what He originally told them to. Nations grew out of the smaller groups of people who spoke the same language.

Four Great Men (Genesis 12–50)

The rest of Genesis is about four important men God chose to be the founders of Israel, His special nation: Abraham, Isaac, Jacob, and Joseph.

God first chose Abraham. Abraham didn't have kids, but God promised that Abraham would have a family that would grow into a big nation and live in a land God gave them. Even though Abraham was old enough to make your grandpa look like a youngster, he believed God's promises, and God called him His friend.

Abraham's son Isaac was next in line, and God gave him the same promise. Then there was Isaac's son Jacob, who had trouble getting along with others. He even wrestled with God! But God still promised Jacob that his family would become a great nation. He gave Jacob a new name: *Israel*.

Jacob had twelve sons, whose children became the twelve tribes of Israel—also called the Israelites. One of his sons, Joseph, was sold into slavery in Egypt by his own brothers. But Joseph trusted God, and God used him to save his family and all of Egypt from a famine.

Why do these men and their families matter? Because God Himself chose them to be His special people—over all the other nations of the world. And it was through this family that Jesus Christ would one day be born and save the world from sin. Israel is part of God's big plan to save anyone who believes in Jesus—including you!

It's easy to think Genesis is just a book of stories you learn about at church. But remember—these stories really happened. God cared about all of these people just like He cares about you.

CULTURE SHOCK

Can you believe that Jacob wrestled God to a standstill (Genesis 32:24-26)? It was more like when you wrestle with your dad. He lets you think you're beating him—until he decides time is up and pins you with ease. God wanted to see if His blessing mattered enough to Jacob to wrestle with Him all night—and it turns out it did!

TOUR GUIDE

- My uncle gave me the choice of the best land around, and I picked a beautiful valley near a city where the residents hated God.
- My wife got salty when she refused to leave our home without looking back.

- I was a righteous man who was bugged by all the messed-up behavior of my neighbors.
- Read Genesis 13, Genesis 19:15-26 and 2 Peter 2:6-8 to find out who I am.

Enjoy Your Trip

Creation Shows You Who God Is

God's creation shows His power, creativity, and beauty. And since you are made in God's image, so do you. He made you just the way you are, and He thinks you're special. As wonderful as His creation is—sunsets, rainbows, tigers, oranges—*you* are even more amazing to Him.

Why Is Sin Such a Big Deal?

Sin is when you choose to do things your way instead of God's way. It separates you from God. Picture a clear, smooth lake that reflects trees and mountains and clouds like a mirror. Sin is like skipping a rock over the surface. It's fun, but it ruins the perfect reflection on the lake. Sin ruins God's image in you.

Where's the Gospel?

After Satan tempted Eve to disobey God, God told Satan, "From now on you and the woman will be enemies, as will your offspring and hers. You will strike his heel, but he will crush your head" (Genesis 3:15 TLB). The "offspring" of the woman is Jesus. In other words, Jesus would one day crush Satan's head. By defeating him at the cross, Jesus would make a way for people to stop sinning and follow God. Even thousands of years before Jesus was born, God told us about the rescue operation He was planning. How awesome is that?

▶ Adam and Eve

Read about their blame game in Genesis 3:8-13.

EXODUS

Check Your Location

Moses wrote the second book of the Bible, Exodus, thousands of years ago. *Exodus* means "going out." Exodus tells how God freed the people of Israel from slavery in Egypt. The Lord wanted the Israelites to go to the land He promised them and start living like they were His people. On the way, He told them how to do that by giving them His law.

EXPECT THE UNEXPECTED

God designed each of the ten plagues to attack a specific Egyptian god or goddess. For example, changing the water in the Nile to blood showed God's superiority to the Egyptian god of the Nile, Hapi. Thoth, the god of wisdom and medicine, was worshipped by throwing the ashes of human sacrifices into the air to bring blessing. So God had Moses throw soot (from a fireplace) in the air. When it came down, people got boils, bringing shame to Thoth. Over and over, God made it clear that He is the one true and living God. Since God is the *only* God, Moses could say, "My God is better than your gods."

Plot Your Course

Slavery in Egypt (Exodus 1–12)

At the beginning of Exodus, Jacob and his family moved to Egypt, where they became known by the name God gave Jacob in Genesis: Israel. Over the next 350 years, the Israelites, also called the Hebrews, grew to around two million people. Egypt's rulers, the pharaohs, made the Hebrews their slaves. However, the Egyptians were afraid that the Israelites would rebel and take over, so one pharaoh ordered all Israelite baby boys to be killed. But God protected one baby named Moses.

When Moses grew up, God spoke to him through a bush that was on fire but didn't burn up! It's hard to ignore a flaming shrub calling your name. The Lord wanted to use Moses to deliver the Israelites and bring them back to their home, the land He had promised Abraham.

So Moses had an epic showdown with Pharaoh. God revealed His power to Egypt through ten plagues that brought all kinds of nastiness down on the Egyptians.

Through it all, Pharaoh refused to let the Israelites go free. The suffering of his own people wasn't enough to make him change his mind, so God had to make it personal: The final plague was the death of all firstborn people and animals.

But God made a way for anyone, whether Hebrew or Egyptian, to be saved. He instructed each family to kill a lamb, smear its blood on the doorframe of their home, and eat a special meal. God then passed over the houses with blood on them, sparing everyone inside. This is what the Jewish people—descendants of the Israelites—still celebrate as *Passover*, a yearly reminder that God delivered them from slavery.

CULTURE SHOCK

The ten plagues were pretty gross! Imagine taking a sip of cool water on a hot Egyptian day only to find your drink has turned to blood. Frogs are cool, but imagine your bed being filled with them. Picture gnats and flies sticking to you all day long. As for the boils, imagine the worst, most painful acne ever—zits from the dark side! And that garden you spent months planting and weeding and taking care of? Gone! Blasted by flaming hail, with the smoking remains scarfed up by a swarm of locusts.

Stuck in the Wilderness (Exodus 13—18)

After that awful final plague, which led to the death of Pharaoh's own son, he basically kicked Israel out of Egypt. Free at last! When the Israelites came to the Red Sea, Moses split the water by God's power. The people walked through on dry ground. Pharaoh sent his army after them, but the water rushed back and wiped them out.

Yet as the Israelites traveled into the desert, they had a hard time trusting the Lord: "Are we there yet?" They grumbled and complained and ran out of provisions: "I'm hunnngrrry!" But God brought them quails to eat, made water come out of a rock, and dropped bread called *manna* from heaven for them each morning.

LEARN THE LANGUAGE—
I AM WHO I AM (Exodus 3:14)

God introduced Himself to Moses by this name. The basic meaning is "I exist." Sounds simple, but the Jews consider God's name so holy that the Hebrew version of this name is just four letters: YHWH. Usually pronounced "Yahweh," this was also a name Jesus used to describe Himself, making it clear that He is God (read John 8:58).

God Gives His Law (Exodus 19—40)

Three months after leaving Egypt, Israel came to Mount Sinai. God called Moses up the mountain and gave him the Law, God's list of rules for how to live. The Ten Commandments, which God wrote Himself on two stone tablets, are a good summary of these rules. The first five tell us how to respect God, and the second five tell us how to respect others.

God gave His people other rules too: how to celebrate holy feasts, how to live a pure life, and how to build a place to worship God—the tabernacle.

Learning all these rules might sound boring. But it actually shows us something cool: God cares about how we live every part our lives. It also shows us something important about God: He is holy. *Holy* means set apart or different. He is completely different than we are because He is perfect and every human being is sinful.

That means no matter how hard the Israelites tried to follow God's law perfectly, they couldn't do it. When Moses came down from Mount Sinai, he found the people worshipping a golden statue they made!

But Moses punished the people, and they turned back to the Lord. Then they built the tabernacle and the Ark of the Covenant, following God's instructions. Once everything was finished, God's glory came to live in the tabernacle. What a great ending!

MUST-SEE SITES—*The Tabernacle*

The tabernacle was like a mobile church (see Exodus 25–27). It was a fence and tent that the Israelites could pack up at a moment's notice and take with them whenever God told them it was time to get moving—which happened a lot in the forty years they were in the wilderness.

TOUR GUIDE

- I had a responsibility to protect my people from any danger, especially the threat of foreign gods.
- I made a lot of big decisions that affected the welfare of a lot of people.
- My stubborn pride cost me the one thing I held closest to my heart.
- Read Exodus 8:24-30, Exodus 10:7, and Exodus 12:29-30 to find out who I am.

Enjoy Your Trip

No More Excuses!

When God first spoke to Moses through the burning bush, Moses made a lot of excuses for why he didn't want to obey God. He was scared. He had a stutter. But God told him, "I created you. Trust Me, and I'll help you." In what ways do you find it hard to obey God? Ask Him for help. He has all the power in the universe.

Nobody's Perfect

Go back and read the Ten Commandments in your Bible (look up Exodus 20:1-17). How many commands have you broken? These rules make it clear that none of us are perfect. But God still loves us! That should make us want to obey what He says.

Where's the Gospel?

The Passover is an awesome picture of salvation. Just like the Israelites used the blood of a lamb to save them from death, so the blood of Jesus, shed on the cross, saved us from sin. The

Bible even calls Jesus a Lamb (check out John 1:29 and 1 Peter 1:19). The blood of the Passover lamb set the Hebrew slaves free, and Jesus Christ the Lamb sets anyone who believes in Him free.

▶ **The Golden Calf**

Read about Moses, Aaron, and the lamest excuse ever in Exodus 32:1-8,15-24.

LEVITICUS

Check Your Location

Moses wrote Leviticus sometime after what happened in Exodus. Leviticus is all about God's rules for His people, the Israelites. Leviticus has two big ideas: (1) how the Israelites could pay for their sins through sacrifice and (2) how the Israelites could become holy, or more like the Lord. God called them to live a certain way and do certain things because they belonged to Him.

LEARN THE LANGUAGE—*Sin* (Leviticus 4:2)

The word used for *sin* was originally used in archery. It described an archer missing his target with his arrow. Whether you sin without knowing it's a sin or you sin and you know it, you are missing the target God has set for you in life.

Plot Your Course

How to Pay Sin's Price (Leviticus 1–17)

God must really hate sin because in Leviticus, God showed His people how to get rid of the penalty of sin. Why does He hate it so much? Because breaking God's rules separates us from Him. He wants a good, close relationship with us. However, sin means that there is a price to pay to have that relationship. God told the Israelites to pay for their sins with the blood of sacrificed animals.

God told the Israelites to worship Him at the tabernacle. He told them to use different animals for different kinds of sacrifices. This included bulls, rams, goats, lambs, and birds. The people could also offer other things, like cakes and grain, but these were optional offerings. They were done out of thankfulness and love to the Lord.

God chose the tribe of Levi to be the priests in charge of the tabernacle. He set one boss, the high priest, over them all. The priests had a serious job. They had to sacrifice the animals. They were the link between the people and God.

In Leviticus, God also told the people how to live by holy habits. This included what animals they were allowed to eat, how to clean themselves, and how to deal with messy things like childbirth and diseases. When they lived according to these rules, it showed the nations around them that they followed God. It also helped them live healthier lives. God knew what He was doing. He wanted to protect His people.

There were also special rules about the Day of Atonement, the most important Hebrew festival. On that special day, the high priest used two goats to show sin's seriousness and God's mercy. He sacrificed Goat #1 as an offering for the whole nation's sin. He let Goat #2 loose in the wilderness to wander off, showing that God had taken their sin away.

CULTURE SHOCK

The old system of sacrifice was bloody. Animals were sacrificed regularly. Their blood was splattered on the sides of the altar in the tabernacle (and later, the temple). Why so much blood? Because blood represents life, and the Bible says the cost of sin is death. Every time the Israelites saw an animal's blood dripping off the altar, they were reminded about the consequences of sin.

EXPECT THE UNEXPECTED

To become a priest, Aaron and his sons had to participate in a strange ceremony. Moses sacrificed a ram, put some of its blood on Aaron and his sons' right ears, right thumbs, and right big toes. Weird, right? Not really. It symbolized their role as priests: The blood on the right ear meant they were called to hear God's voice. The blood on the right thumb meant they were called to do His will. And the blood on the right big toe meant they were called to walk in His ways.

How to Be Holy (Leviticus 18–27)

The rest of Leviticus describes how the Israelites could become holy. *Holy* means different, unique, set apart, or devoted to God. God is holy, but how can a person be holy? It means they live differently because they follow God and His rules. That means *you* can be holy! And God wants you to be. He said, "Be holy, for I am holy" (Leviticus 11:45 TLB).

God knows what makes life work best. He gave the Israelites certain rules because He loved them. He does the same for you and me. God gave them rules about husbands and wives, families, priests, workers, and farmers. He also told them to joyfully celebrate the feasts of Passover, Pentecost, and Tabernacles. Each of these feasts was like a party for the whole nation and reminded the Israelites of all that God had done for them.

When Israel lived according to the laws in Leviticus, they looked different from the other nations around them. Today, we don't have to follow the laws in Leviticus anymore. God still gives us rules, but now Jesus helps us follow them!

TOUR GUIDE

- My brother was a big shot in Israel, but I spoke up for God in front of Pharaoh.
- I had one of the most important jobs in all of Israel, but it meant getting blood all over my work clothes.
- Two of my sons dishonored God and died as a result.
- Read Exodus 4:14-17, Leviticus 8:20, and Leviticus 10:1-3 to find out who I am.

Enjoy Your Trip

Taking Care of Your Body

A lot of God's law deals with the human body—what to eat, how to treat sickness, and how to stay clean. God wants you to take care of your body. Be thankful that God cares about every detail of your life.

Celebrating What God Has Done

It's good to celebrate what God has done for you and your friends and family. When God told the Israelites to hold feast days, He *commanded* them to rejoice (Leviticus 23:40). Why would God need to tell someone to be happy? God knew that life is hard sometimes, so He wanted the people to have some fun. Look up Psalms 95:1, 98:4, and 100:1-2. We're supposed to *shout* out how awesome God is! Do you celebrate the Lord?

Where's the Gospel?

The Israelites had to sacrifice animals for their sins over and over again. But we don't have to sacrifice animals anymore because of Jesus Christ. When He died on the cross, His blood covered all our sins forever. God accepted Jesus's blood as payment because Jesus kept all of God's rules perfectly. All the sacrifices of Leviticus pointed to Jesus's once-and-for-all sacrifice on the cross. Aren't you glad we don't have to sacrifice animals anymore?

NUMBERS

Check Your Location

Numbers was the fourth book in the Bible written by Moses. It tells us about the almost forty years Israel roamed in the desert after they left Egypt and before they entered the Promised Land, the land God promised Abraham. The book of Numbers isn't named after your math homework but after two censuses, or numberings, of the Israelite people.

MUST-SEE SITES—
The Wilderness of Sinai (Numbers 1:1)

The first place Israel camped after escaping Egypt was sun-scorched and barren. In places, giant rocky cliffs surrounded narrow valleys. Water, food, and plants were rare, but scorpions and snakes were not. It's easy to see why the Israelites complained about being there. But the whole point was for them to learn to trust the God who brought them out of slavery in Egypt. God provided everything they needed, even if it wasn't everything they wanted. Only God could have kept them alive the whole time they were there.

Plot Your Course

Counting the People (Numbers 1–4)

Two years after God brought Israel out of Egypt, He told

Moses to count the people. It may not seem exciting, but all the names and numbers listed show us something special: God loves and cares about every single one of His people, including you! You're much more than a number!

God then gave directions for the different duties the priests needed to do in the tabernacle, the special tent where God's presence stayed.

The Israelites weren't in the Promised Land yet, so they lived a wandering, or nomadic, lifestyle. They moved when God told them to move. At first, they were obedient and faithful when following the Lord.

Correcting the Problems (Numbers 5–25)

But the Hebrews began to grumble. They had seen God do so many miracles, but that was the problem—they got too used to seeing amazing things! They started complaining that God wasn't taking care of them well enough even though He traveled with them and gave them water, food, and shelter. He also kept their clothes from wearing out!

When the Israelites came to the edge of the Promised Land, they sent a dozen men to spy out the land. The spies reported that the land had everything they needed, but they were terrified of the people who already lived there. Only *two guys*—Caleb and Joshua—believed God would help them. The rest were scared and complained again.

This made God angry, but Moses begged God to be merciful. So God made a promise that only the kids of the Israelites—along with Caleb and Joshua—would be allowed to enter the Promised Land. Everyone else would die in the wilderness. What a sad price to pay!

As time went on, the people grumbled about not having water. God told Moses to talk to a rock to make water come out of it. Instead, Moses yelled at the Israelites and hit the rock with his staff—really hard. Water still came out, but Moses hadn't followed God's instructions. As a consequence, God didn't let Moses enter the Promised Land. God takes sin seriously!

Then the Israelites started complaining *again*. This time, God was done with their whining. He sent a bunch of snakes into the camp to bite and kill those who complained. Moses prayed for the people, and God had Moses put a metal snake on top of a pole. Whoever looked at it was healed. It sounds strange, but it worked.

As the Hebrews wandered in the wilderness, the people battled and defeated their enemies with God's help. One king named Balak was scared of Israel, so he hired a man named Balaam to curse Israel. God told Balaam to bless Israel instead, and he did.

Yet Balaam tempted the Israelites to sin in another way. Some of them began to worship Baal, a fake god. God was not happy. He sent a plague that killed 24,000 people! But many more Israelites than that died in the wilderness. That was the consequence of the people's unbelief in God.

LEARN THE LANGUAGE— *Purify*
(Numbers 19:12)

If *sin* means you've missed the target, to purify yourself is to make it possible to hit it. The rules God gave Moses showed various ways someone could be made pure—by offering a sacrifice, making another kind of offering, or pouring special water or oil over themselves. But the only way to be made pure is to confess sin, trust Jesus to make you a new person, and stop sinning.

Continuing the Journey (Numbers 26—36)

After thirty-seven years, it was time to count the people again. This *numbering* was because all the older Israelites had died. Their children had grown up and were ready to start a new life in the Promised Land.

Moses reminded this new generation about God's rules for living. Then God helped the people defeat their enemies and cross the Jordan River. They finally arrived in the Promised Land, and each tribe of Israel got their share of the land.

Did you know it should have taken only eleven days to get to the Promised Land from Egypt? But Israel took almost forty years. They didn't believe God would take care of them and got lost as a result. They messed up big time! But God didn't give up on them—and He doesn't give up on you and me either.

TOUR GUIDE

- I was hired to place a curse on a huge group of people who were invading a king's lands.
- My donkey and I had an argument about the way I treated him after he crushed my foot against a wall. The donkey won.
- Every time I tried to curse these people, blessings came out instead, which made the guy who hired me really mad.
- Read Numbers 22:5-6, Numbers 22:21-33, and Numbers 24:9-13 to find out who I am.

Enjoy Your Trip

Complaining

The Israelites complained a lot. It makes God sad when you

complain because it tells Him that you don't think He'll take care of you. What do you complain about? How can you be thankful to the Lord instead? Do you trust that God will help you even when things are hard or scary?

Where's the Gospel?

The bronze snake on a pole is a symbol of Jesus Christ. Jesus said, "As Moses lifted up the bronze snake on a pole in the wilderness, so the Son of Man [Jesus] must be lifted up, so that everyone who believes in him will have eternal life" (John 3:14-15). Jesus was lifted up off the ground on the cross. And whoever looks to Him and believes in Him will be saved from the bite of sin and death.

▶ Balaam

Read about his talking donkey in Numbers 22:21-31.

DEUTERONOMY

Check Your Location

Like the first four books of the Bible, Deuteronomy was written by Moses (except for the last chapter, which tells how he died). It takes place right before the people of Israel entered the Promised Land. *Deuteronomy* means "second law" because Moses gave the people three farewell speeches that repeated God's law and reminded them of the most important parts.

Plot Your Course

Moses's First Speech (Deuteronomy 1–3)

Moses began by reminding the people of the cost of their disobedience to God. Because they kept disobeying Him, they had to wander for almost forty years in the desert. That delayed them from entering the Promised Land. Then Moses went over laws and past events, explaining things from his point of view.

The number of Hebrews who had died in the wilderness was around 1,200,000. That means they had about eighty-five funerals every day! It was a reminder that the price of sin—disobeying the Lord—is death.

Moses's Second Speech (Deuteronomy 4–26)

Moses then gave the people rules for how to live right in the Promised Land. He went back over all the laws from Exodus, Leviticus, and Numbers. The new generation needed to hear

God's truth again and know what He wanted them to do so they could pass it on to their children.

This included following a very important commandment: "You must love the LORD your God with all your heart, all your soul, and all your strength" (Deuteronomy 6:5). This is the rule Jesus called "the first and greatest commandment" (Matthew 22:38). When you love God above everything else, you will *want* to obey all His other rules.

PACK SMART

Moses warned the Israelites that not everyone who says they are speaking for God really is. Some people say they have a message from God, but if they tell you to do things that the Bible says you shouldn't, don't listen to them. Moses said times like that are a test from God to see "if you truly love him with all your heart and soul" (Deuteronomy 13:3).

LEARN THE LANGUAGE—*Humble*

Being humble doesn't mean being shy. It means putting others before yourself. Most people are not naturally humble, but prideful instead. We can learn to be humble by putting God first in our lives. We're being humble when we obey Him, especially when He tells us to put others ahead of ourselves (see Deuteronomy 8:2).

Moses's Third Speech (Deuteronomy 27–30)

In Moses's final message, he told the people that when they entered the Promised Land, they were to find large stones, paint them white, and write the law on them. These rocks would be a monument and help remind them of how to live whenever they saw it.

Then Moses reminded the people that *if* they obeyed the Lord, He would bless them abundantly. But *if* they disobeyed Him, curses would come on them. We call this a conditional covenant. The promises of God's blessings were based on the *condition* of their obedience. If they didn't obey—no blessings.

Moses ended by telling the Israelites that God gave them all these rules because He loved them. God wanted to be near them and have a relationship with them, but He could only do that if they obeyed His law.

LEARN THE LANGUAGE—*Covenant* (Deuteronomy 4:13)

A covenant is an agreement that benefits both sides. Moses spoke of the Ten Commandments as God's covenant with Israel. That's a conditional covenant. It has two parts: the part God does and the part you do. If they obeyed God's laws, He would bless them. Another covenant, the one God made with Abraham, was unconditional. That means God did all the work: He promised the land to Abraham and his descendants for all time.

Taking a Break (Deuteronomy 31–34)

Moses's time on earth was up. Because he had disobeyed God in the book of Numbers, he wasn't allowed to enter the Promised Land. But the people were in good hands: God was with them.

God also gave the Hebrews a new leader: Joshua. Moses encouraged and blessed Joshua. Then he shared a song with the people. I don't know how the tune went, but old man Moses sang a lot about Israel's disobedience and failures.

However, Moses's final words in the Bible were full of happiness. He blessed all the tribes of Israel and said goodbye. Then God took Moses to Mount Nebo and showed him the Promised Land. Moses died up on the mountain. He was 120 years old.

The Israelites (and their descendants, the Jews) remembered Moses as a mighty man of God for thousands of years after his death, even until today.

MUST-SEE SITES—*Mount Nebo*

Mount Nebo overlooks the Promised Land. From its peak, on a clear day, God showed Moses the whole land, including the walled city of Jericho, the Dead Sea, and the place where Jerusalem would later be built. Moses spent his last few days on Nebo, but no one has ever found his body or even a grave.

Enjoy Your Trip

Don't Forget!

In Deuteronomy, Moses repeated a lot of what God already told the Israelites. Moses said, "Be careful not to forget the Lord." God wanted His people to take the time to remember Him. What do you do to remember the Lord? List what God has done for you—all His blessings—and what He wants you to do (based on what the Bible says).

God's Rules Are for Our Good

Moses told the Israelites, "Choose life, so that you and your descendants might live! You can make this choice by loving the LORD your God, obeying him, and committing yourself firmly to him. This is the key to your life" (Deuteronomy 30:19-20).

God gave His people the law because He wanted them to have life. God doesn't give rules to be mean. He gives rules because He knows what's best for us. After all, He made us!

Where's the Gospel?

Moses made a prediction: "The LORD your God will raise up for you a prophet like me from among your fellow Israelites. You must listen to him" (Deuteronomy 18:15). Bible scholars believe this "prophet" is Jesus Christ. So Moses himself was a lot like Jesus. Pretty cool, right?

JOSHUA

Check Your Location

After Moses died, God chose Moses's assistant, Joshua, as Israel's new leader. Joshua became like an army general who led the nation to conquer the Promised Land, also called Canaan. For the first time, we get to see the Hebrews live in their own land—the land God promised Abraham. Joshua himself wrote this book, except for the end, which records his death.

Plot Your Course

Entering the Land (Joshua 1–5)

Along with his buddy Caleb, Joshua had spied out Canaan years before and wanted the people to take it. Now God told Joshua to go for it. Everywhere the people went, God would give the land to them.

Joshua sent some spies to scout out Jericho, the first city in their path. The spies stayed with a woman named Rahab, who hid them from the city authorities. She believed in God and asked for her and her family to be protected when Israel invaded.

Joshua's spies returned with a good report: The people of the land were scared of the Israelites. The time had come to enter the land. So God split the waters of the Jordan River so the people could pass through, just like He did years earlier with the Red Sea.

Then the Israelites had to take care of some unfinished business. They celebrated the Passover feast and made sure they were following all of God's rules. They were finally ready in mind, body, and spirit to enter the land.

Taking the Land (Joshua 6—12)

As Israel prepared to attack Jericho, Joshua met the mysterious commander of God's armies, a "man" with a sword. Joshua wanted to fight, but this commander told him to worship first. Some scholars think that this commander was none other than Jesus Himself!

Then God told Joshua how to defeat the walled city of Jericho. Led by the priests, the people marched around the city for seven days. It was a strange strategy, but it worked. On the seventh day, when the priests blew their trumpets and the people shouted, the walls of the city fell down!

God continued to give Israel victory over their enemies in Canaan. But He never let them take credit for their victories. It was all the Lord. The people fought for a total of seven years to conquer the land.

MUST-SEE SITES—*Jericho*

The first city Israel conquered after entering the Promised Land was called Jericho. Big cities back then had enormous walls around them for protection. Only God could have brought down Jericho's walls, and He did so without the Israelites having to lift a finger.

CULTURE SHOCK

At Joshua's request, God made the sun stand still in the sky for twenty-four hours, giving Israel's army enough time to defeat their enemy (Joshua 10:12-14). It sounds crazy, but remember—if God made everything, He can control everything.

Living in the Land (Joshua 12—24)

Then it took eighteen years for Israel to spread out and settle in the land. There were twelve separate groups, called "tribes," and they had to keep moving until they found their plot of land. The rest of the book gives lots of details about how much land each tribe got. Joshua was now old—he was in his eighties! But he still helped the people settle in the land.

After so long, God had kept His promise to Abraham. Even though God had given them victory and a land of their own, the Israelites didn't fully obey Him. God told them to kick all the local people out of the land. But instead of kicking out the Canaanites, the Israelites let them stay. They even made the Canaanites their slaves. Because the Israelites didn't obey God all the way, the Canaanites caused a lot of trouble later on.

Joshua chose a place called Shiloh to be the Israelites' headquarters for the next 400 years. It was here that the people put that tent called the tabernacle, Israel's special place of worship to God.

Finally, there was peace in the land. The time came for Joshua to say goodbye to the people before he died. He told them that the best reason to serve God was because of everything God had done for them. So the people committed themselves to God.

LEARN THE LANGUAGE—*Hold Firmly*

Joshua told the Israelites to "hold firmly" to God (Joshua 22:5). In Hebrew, "hold firmly" is one word, and it means to stick with someone no matter what—like they are a firefighter leading you out of a burning building.

Enjoy Your Trip

Making the Walls Fall Down

Think of how funny it must have looked to the people in Jericho to see the Israelite army march around their city day after day but never fight. But God showed His strength on the seventh day. Have you ever been afraid of doing the right thing because of how it might look to other people? God can help you do it if you will just obey Him.

Kicking Out the Canaanites

Why did Israel have to kick out the Canaanites? Because the Canaanites worshipped false gods and practiced horrible things. That would be a bad influence on the Israelites. Even a little bit of sin in your life will grow and be harmful to you if you don't kick it out.

Where's the Gospel?

The name *Joshua* is a different version of the name *Jesus*. Joshua brought the people into the land and helped them find peace. In the same way, Jesus made things right between us and God and also gave us peace.

TOUR GUIDE

- I had a sketchy background in Jericho, but I believed in God, and He saved me.
- I am listed as an ancestor of Jesus and in the Hall of Faith in Hebrews.
- Read Joshua 2, Matthew 1:5, and Hebrews 11:31 to find out who I am.

▶ Caleb in the Promised Land

Read about an eighty-five-year-old champion in Joshua 14:6-15.

JUDGES

Check Your Location

We don't know exactly who wrote Judges or when. But the book tells us what happened in the 350 years after Joshua died. Mostly, the Israelites messed up a lot. They did the same thing over and over again: First, they would disobey the Lord. Then God let the nations around them take them captive. Finally, they would turn back to God, and He would send a special leader, called a judge, to set them free. That's where the name *Judges* comes from: the fifteen different leaders who helped Israel during this time.

Plot Your Course

A Good Start Goes Bad (Judges 1–16)

After Joshua died, the people of Israel got off to a good start. They did what God told them to, and God kept giving them victory over the Canaanites, helping them conquer the Promised Land.

But as soon as the Israelites started disobeying the Lord, things got really bad really quickly. They didn't completely drive out the Canaanites like God told them to. They forgot how God helped them in the past, so they didn't trust God to help them now. They began to lose battles. Their old enemies, the Canaanites, started driving *them* out of the land!

PACK SMART

The pattern of sin in Judges is called the sin cycle. It's like a big circle where people sin, and then God gives them consequences. Then they're sorry and ask God to forgive them, and He does. Then He helps them get out of the trouble they got themselves in.

When you sin, you might not get in trouble right away. But if you keep sinning, you will definitely get in trouble at some point. You hurt yourself and other people when you sin, but more than that, your sin hurts God. It moves you away from Him. He hates to see that happen, so be quick to break any sin cycles in your life and get back to doing things God's way.

A Vicious Cycle

The Israelites stopped worshipping God and started worshipping the fake gods of the people who lived around them. So God stopped protecting Israel and let their enemies capture them. When Israel finally cried out to God for help, God sent them a judge to rescue them. But once the Israelites were home safe, they decided to stop following the Lord again.

The people did this seven more times! Seven times they disobeyed God. Seven times other nations made them their slaves. And seven times the Lord sent a judge to help free them.

The judges were often the least likely people to be leaders, but that's how God works.

- Ehud was a left-handed fighter, which was rare. He was able to sneak in and assassinate a tyrant king who had conquered and ruled Israel (Judges 3:15-30).
- The only woman judge, Deborah, was tough! She led

Israel's general and his army of Israelites into battle (Judges 4:4-14).
- Gideon was a weak, scared man. But God called him to lead an army of only 300 Israelites against the enemy's army of 135,000 (Judges 7:7-9,15-22). And Israel won!

Probably the most famous judge is Samson. Samson had the strength of a superhero, only he was *real*! But he was more interested in doing what he wanted to do. He was selfish and violent. Yet God still used him to defeat Israel's enemies.

Eventually, Samson's bad ways caught up with him. His girlfriend, Delilah, gave away the secret of his strength to Israel's enemies. Samson became weak, and his enemies captured and blinded him. But right before he died, God gave him his strength back so he could defeat those same enemies.

CULTURE SHOCK

For a hero, Samson did a lot of really strange things. One time, he killed a lion. Later, he passed by the lion's corpse, saw that bees had made a hive in it, and ate some of the honey! Another time, he got mad at some people, so he caught 300 foxes, tied their tails together, and then tied torches between their tails and set them loose. They burned up all the fields of the people Samson was mad at. Not very heroic!

Sad Times (Judges 17—21)

Judges ends on a sad note: "In those days Israel had no king; all the people did whatever seemed right in their own eyes" (Judges 21:25). When we do what *we* think is right—instead of following what *God* says is right—bad things happen.

> **LEARN THE LANGUAGE—*Honorable***
> Often in Judges, the Israelites did not act "honorably" (Judges 9:16,19). To be honorable means that you do the right thing, no matter what. God will take care of anyone who honors His name and His ways.

Enjoy Your Trip

God Likes and Employs Weirdos

God chose many different people to be His judges. He often chooses people you don't expect to be His heroes. If you want to be used by God, He just wants you to be willing to do what He says. You don't need any special talent. Just tell God, "I'm available if You want to put me to work."

God Never Gives Up on You

God was sick of the Israelites' sin, but He never gave up on them. And He never gives up on you and me either. Even when you sin and mess up over and over again, God still loves you. His love doesn't depend on whether you obey Him, even though He still wants you to do what He says. But He wants you to obey because you love Him too and want to please Him.

Where's the Gospel?

God sent the judges to save the Israelites from being slaves to their enemies. Later, God sent Jesus Christ to deliver us from being slaves to sin. We can't stop doing bad things on our own, and we need someone stronger than us to deliver us. That someone is Jesus.

RUTH

Check Your Location

The story of Ruth took place during the time of the judges, those special leaders we read about in the previous chapter. We don't know exactly who wrote Ruth, but the book is a love story. Before you say "Yuck!" you need to know Ruth isn't just about a man and woman falling in love. It's also about the love a daughter showed her adopted mom. Ruth is one of only two books in the Bible named after a woman. It's also the only book named after an ancestor of Jesus Christ!

Plot Your Course

Surviving the Famine (Ruth 1)

A woman from Israel named Naomi was living in Moab when some terrible things happened to her. Her husband and both her grown sons died. Not only that, but there was also a famine in the land.

Naomi decided to return to Israel because she heard the Lord had blessed His people with good crops. But she told her son's wives to stay in Moab, where they could remarry among their own people. But one of them, named Ruth, wanted to stay with Naomi. Ruth committed herself to Naomi. She even decided to worship the God Naomi worshipped: the God of Israel. So the two women traveled to Bethlehem, where Naomi was from.

Working the Fields (Ruth 2)

One of Naomi's relatives, Boaz, owned land around Bethlehem. One day, Boaz saw Ruth gathering grain in his field. Boaz had heard her story and wanted to help her.

Ruth just wanted to work in the fields so she could get food for Naomi. She wasn't expecting to be helped by Boaz, especially since she wasn't an Israelite, but a foreigner. Still, Boaz went above and beyond in his kindness to Ruth. He let her gather the best grain from his fields.

Making a Match (Ruth 3)

Naomi went into matchmaker mode. She told Ruth to get washed up and put on perfume and then go to Boaz in the evening and see if he would marry Ruth.

Wait—the girl asked the guy? Yes! This is what God said to do in His law. If a husband died before he had a kid, his wife would marry a close relative. Then the two of them would have a family. This was so that the first husband's family would keep going in Israel.

Boaz knew all this. And he agreed to marry Ruth!

Marrying the Man (Ruth 4)

Boaz followed all the details of the law in order to marry Ruth properly. So Boaz and Ruth got married. Naomi had a happy ending too. Even though her husband and sons died, she found a true and loving daughter in Ruth.

It may not sound like our kind of fairy-tale ending, but it was for Naomi, Ruth, and Boaz.

Why is the story of Ruth important to you and me? It shows us that God works out good things in our normal, everyday lives. When you go to school or your parents go to work, God is doing His work as well.

LEARN THE LANGUAGE—*Redeem*

Redeem is an important word in the Bible. It means to buy something back that used to belong to you. Boaz bought back land that used to belong to Naomi's family so they could have a home (Ruth 4:4-12). Jesus bought you back from being a slave to sin, so you could have a home with Him.

Enjoy Your Trip

God Can Use Anyone

Ruth wasn't an Israelite. She was from Moab. The Moabites were enemies of Israel and worshipped a false god. But Ruth chose to worship the true God and became part of Jesus's family tree. It doesn't matter what country, city, or family you come from; God still loves you, and He can use you to do awesome things!

Kindness Goes a Long Way

Ruth's name means "friendship," and she was a true friend to Naomi. Being friendly and kind helps all your relationships run smoothly, whether it's with your parents, siblings, friends, classmates, or teachers. How can you show kindness to those around you?

Where's the Gospel?

Ruth and Boaz's first child, Obed, was King David's grandfather! And do you know who eventually came from King David's family line? Jesus Christ. Even though Ruth wasn't an Israelite, she got to be part of Jesus's family tree. How cool is that? Eventually, Jesus Christ was born in Bethlehem (according to a prophecy in Micah 5:2). And Bethlehem was the very city where Naomi, Ruth, and Boaz lived!

1 AND 2 SAMUEL

Check Your Location

The books of 1 and 2 Samuel were originally one book. The prophet Samuel may have written the book, or he may have just collected all the information and put it in a book. It tells the story of the prophet Samuel and the first two kings of Israel, Saul and David. These three men lived thousands of years ago, but they were people just like you and me. God chose them to help lead His nation, and they did some great things—and some not-so-great things.

1 SAMUEL

Plot Your Course

The Prophet Samuel (1 Samuel 1–8)

After the gloomy time of the judges, Israel didn't have any leaders, so God called on a young boy named Samuel. When Samuel got a little older—about your age—he went to the tabernacle to learn how to serve God there.

God introduced Himself to Samuel one night. He told him to be His new priest and prophet. A prophet was someone who heard from God and then told the people what God said. God didn't care that Samuel was so young. He saw Samuel's heart and knew Samuel wanted to serve Him.

Samuel grew up and was a faithful priest and prophet to Israel. But the people saw that all the other nations around them had kings. One day they said, "C'mon, Sam, we want a king!" God decided to give them what they wanted even though having a king would make things a lot harder for them than they expected.

Saul, the First King (1 Samuel 9—15)

God appointed a man named Saul to be Israel's first king. He was tall and handsome, and he was from a good family. So Samuel anointed him, which means he smeared olive oil on Saul to mark him as a king.

Saul started out as a humble king, but then he became arrogant and full of himself. He even disobeyed some of God's direct orders. Later on, Saul said, "I have been a fool and very, very wrong" (1 Samuel 26:21).

That couldn't be truer! God eventually became fed up with Saul. God let him stay on the throne for a while, but He had rejected him as king and planned to replace him.

David, the Second King (1 Samuel 16—31)

God told Samuel to pick one of the sons of a man named Jesse as the next king. God chose the least likely son: the youngest, David—a shepherd and musician. God explained why He chose David: "Men judge by outward appearance, but I look at a man's thoughts and intentions" (1 Samuel 16:7 TLB). In his heart, David was very different from Saul. He was truly humble, and he loved God.

David came to be known as a great warrior. His most famous warrior moment was when he defeated the Philistine giant, Goliath. Goliath was nine feet tall, with a spear that was almost as long and had a seventeen-pound iron tip! But David took a sling and some rocks and killed Goliath in God's name. That made David famous in Israel.

King Saul soon became jealous of David. He came to hate David so much that he even tried to kill him—more than once! So David had to go on the run and live as a fugitive. But God was with David. Saul's son Jonathan, who was best friends with David, helped him too.

Through it all, David did not fight back against Saul even when he had the chance. Saul was still the king, and David respected that. During this time, David wrote some of the Psalms—poetic songs about how God helped him in his life.

In the end, Saul was killed in a battle with the Philistines, ancient enemies of Israel. It was a sad ending. The main thing the book of 1 Samuel shows us is the difference between Saul and David: Saul chose to live selfishly. David chose to serve God.

CULTURE SHOCK

The Israelites and Philistines were always fighting each other. One time, the Philistines won and captured the Ark of the Covenant, the holy box that contained the Ten Commandments God gave Moses. But when they brought it home as a victory trophy, God punished them for their disrespect. A few days after they put the Ark in their temple, a statue of their god Dagon fell over in front of it like it was bowing down to God! Then the presence of the Ark gave the Philistines hemorrhoids. It got so bad that they gave the Ark back to Israel along with an offering of five gold mice and—this is crazy!—five pieces of gold shaped like hemorrhoids (1 Samuel 5–6).

Enjoy Your Trip

You Don't Always Get What You Want

The Israelites whined until they got what they wanted: a king.

But Saul ended up being a horrible king. When you want something that everyone else has, God might not choose to give it to you. That might be because He's protecting you. He always knows what's best for you!

Where's the Gospel?

King David was the ancestor of Jesus Christ, the King of kings. David was also from Bethlehem and the tribe of Judah, just like Jesus. Jesus is sometimes even called the *Son of David* (Matthew 20:30).

▶ David and Goliath

Read about the world's greatest underdog in 1 Samuel 17:1-10,32-51.

2 SAMUEL

Plot Your Course

David's Victories (2 Samuel 1—10)

Saul and his sons died in battle with the Philistines. After mourning their deaths, David officially became the king of Judah, the southern part of the country of Israel.

It took seven years for David to be made king over all of Israel. Then he conquered the city of Jerusalem and made it the center of Israel, which it still is today. David also had lots of kids with his wives (yes, he had more than one wife...*not okay, David!*).

David moved the Ark of the Covenant and the tabernacle, the place of God's worship, to Jerusalem. There was a celebration with lots of people singing and dancing. Israel was finally at peace.

Then David had an idea: He wanted to build God a real temple instead of a cloth tent like the one they had for many years. God responded through His prophet, Nathan, "I don't really care about having a big house. But I am going to build *you* a house that will last forever." By "house," God meant a big line of descendants. David was overwhelmed by God's goodness to him.

TOUR GUIDE

- I was the son of the king, but I was best friends with the man who replaced him.
- I helped my friend get away from my dad, who wanted to kill him.
- I died in battle, and my friend wrote a song to honor me.
- Read 1 Samuel 18:1-3, 1 Samuel 19:1-2, and 2 Samuel 1:17-27 to find out who I am.

PACK SMART

When David had defeated all his enemies, he went to search for any living relatives of Jonathan, his best friend. Jonathan had died years before, but David wanted to honor him. Sure enough, Jonathan had a son named Mephibosheth, who was crippled. David took Mephibosheth to live in his palace and let him dine at his own royal table (2 Samuel 9). David had nothing to gain from taking care of the guy. But David wanted to do what was right anyway.

David's Mistakes (2 Samuel 11—12)

The Lord blessed David, but that didn't mean David was perfect. One spring, Israel's army went out to battle, but David stayed home in Jerusalem. When he saw a beautiful woman bathing on a rooftop, he didn't look away like he should have. Instead, he found the woman, whose name was Bathsheba. David took her as his wife even though she was already married.

Bathsheba ended up getting pregnant with David's child. David tried to cover up the whole thing by having her husband killed in battle. God is never happy when it comes to our sin, even with someone like David.

David's Family Drama (2 Samuel 13—24)

David wasn't the only one who struggled with sin. His whole family was a mess. One of David's grown-up sons, Absalom, killed his own half brother!

Then Absalom became so angry at his dad that he decided to kick him off the throne. Absalom gathered some people and invaded Jerusalem, which forced his dad, David, to go on the run.

Eventually, David and his army came against Absalom and his men. Absalom died while running away from the battle. Absalom's rebellion was just the beginning of the trouble Israel would see in the future.

The book of 2 Samuel ends with God telling David to build Him an altar near Jerusalem. The land David bought was a threshing floor—a flat, rock-hard surface where wheat was beaten and separated into grain and chaff (the leftover husks). People ate the grain and threw away the chaff. This particular threshing floor was a special spot. It would be the place where David's son Solomon would build God's temple.

Enjoy Your Trip

Sin Hurts God

It took a long time for David to confess his sin with Bathsheba. To confess means to tell God that you messed up and sinned against Him. David told God, "It is against you and you alone I sinned and did this terrible thing" (Psalm 51:4 TLB). You can—and should—be sorry when your sin hurts other people.

But when you sin, you're breaking God's law first and foremost, and it hurts Him. That's why it's so important to confess your sin to Him. God already knows you messed up. He just wants to hear you admit it. He is ready to forgive you when you do!

Where's the Gospel?

God promised there would be a long line of kings related to David. Almost all the kings came and went a long time ago. But one was yet to arrive: Jesus Christ. Jesus is a descendant of David, and He was born in Bethlehem and died in Jerusalem. But He rose from the dead, and one day He will return and rule from Jerusalem.

MUST-SEE SITES—
Araunah's Threshing Floor

God told David to purchase a threshing floor from a guy named Araunah (2 Samuel 24:18-25). He wanted David to build an altar for worshipping God there. A threshing floor was a smooth, hard piece of ground where harvested grain was separated from the straw and husks so it could be eaten.

This wasn't just any old threshing floor, though. This location was special to God. Centuries before, Abraham had offered his son Isaac at that same spot. David's son Solomon would build the temple there. And almost 500 years after that, Jesus would be crucified nearby. God had all that in mind when He picked out the spot. Pretty cool, right?

LEARN THE LANGUAGE—*Truth*

David said to God, "Your words are truth" (2 Samuel 7:28). For a lot of people, truth is based on what they feel is right. That means that truth depends on how they're feeling at the moment—happy, sad, angry. But God's truth never changes. That's because God never changes. He is always perfect and good and right. So when you read the Bible, you are reading God's words, and they are true. You can trust them, rely on them, and take comfort from them.

1 AND 2 KINGS

Check Your Location

The book of 1 Kings is a story about Israel's kings. It covers about 130 years of history, starting with King David's son Solomon. Solomon built God a temple and made the nation richer than it had ever been. But even though Israel grew strong outwardly, they grew weak spiritually. They rebelled against God and started worshipping idols—false gods. Then after Solomon died, Israel split into two different nations (Israel and Judah) with two different kings.

Second Kings tells us about all the kings who ruled Israel and Judah during this time. There were a few good kings, but most of them? Flops! Because so many of their kings forgot about God and disrespected Him, Israel was eventually conquered by their enemies. Then many years later, because of the same kind of bad leadership, Judah fell to their enemies too.

1 KINGS

Plot Your Course

A United Kingdom (1 Kings 1—11)

At the end of David's life, he anointed his son Solomon as king. Then David died. He had reigned over Israel for forty years.

Solomon loved and followed the Lord. So one night, God talked to Solomon in a dream and told him to ask for anything he wanted. Solomon had a lot of responsibility as the new king. He wanted to be a good ruler, so he asked God for wisdom. God was very pleased with Solomon's request. He also gave him wealth, honor, respect, and an understanding heart.

One of Solomon's biggest achievements was building Jerusalem's first temple for the worship of God. Many people worked on the project—183,000 in total! It took seven years to build, and it was twice the size of the tabernacle. It was made with the best materials that today would be worth billions of dollars!

After Solomon put the Ark of the Covenant and all the furnishings that had been in the tabernacle inside, God's glory filled the temple.

But even though Solomon was very wise, he wasn't perfect. Solomon taxed the Israelite people too much. He spent twice as long building his own palace as he spent building God's temple. And he had 700 wives—and 300 other women he wasn't even married to! *That's insane!*

PACK SMART

The queen of Sheba came all the way from Africa to visit Solomon because she heard about his wisdom. She was blown away by what she heard and saw! She must have been wise herself, traveling all that way to learn from someone who could teach her how to be a better leader.

A Divided Kingdom (1 Kings 12—22)

Many of those 1,000 women were not from Israel. They turned Solomon's heart away from God to follow the false gods they grew up with. So God said He would take away the kingdom from Solomon.

When Solomon died, the kingdom split. Originally, Israel

had been twelve tribes. But now, one man ruled the ten northern tribes, who called themselves Israel. Another man ruled the two southern tribes, who called themselves Judah.

The rest of 1 Kings tells the two separate stories of these kingdoms and their kings. All of these kings are also mentioned in 1 and 2 Chronicles (the next two books in the Bible).

Israel and Judah fought each other regularly. Not only that, but all of Israel's kings were horrible. Only two of Judah's kings did what was right. God was being very patient during these years.

One of Israel's kings was really bad. Ahab and his wife, Jezebel, worshipped a fake god called Baal. So God sent a prophet named Elijah to Israel to tell them it was wrong.

Elijah set up a contest against all of Baal's fake prophets (850 in total). First, they called on Baal all day to send fire and burn up a sacrificed bull. But nothing happened. Then Elijah poured *water* on his bull and asked God to do the same thing. *Foosh!* Fire fell from heaven and burned it all up!

Even after this awesome victory, Elijah got scared when Jezebel threatened to kill him. But God reminded Elijah that he wasn't alone against the evil queen. There were still people left in Israel who worshipped God. Elijah was encouraged and got back in the fight.

LEARN THE LANGUAGE—
The Name of the Lord

Both Solomon and Elijah called on the name of the Lord to honor God and ask for His help. When you hear the name of God, think of His goodness and how trustworthy He is. Think of His love and His desire to help you be the best person you can be. You can always call on Him! When you learn to pray daily, you'll become wiser.

Enjoy Your Trip

Wise but Dumb

Despite his wisdom, Solomon broke almost all of God's guidelines for kings. He started out great but ended badly. That's because he didn't spend time reading about those rules in God's Word. Do you spend time reading about what God wants you to do in the Bible? You can be the wisest person in the world, but if you don't do what God tells you to, that's pretty dumb!

Where's the Gospel?

Did you know Jesus said He was "greater than Solomon" (Matthew 12:42)? Solomon had loads of wealth and wisdom. But one day in the future, Jesus will outshine Solomon in wisdom and glory. Jesus will show the entire world how great He is and rule over everything!

▶ Elijah and the Prophets of Baal

Read about this "Baal fail" in 1 Kings 18:20-39.

2 KINGS

Plot Your Course

The Struggling Kingdoms (2 Kings 1–17)

After the country split, the people and their kings chose to worship idols and live wickedly. So God sent the prophets Elijah and Elisha to get them back on track.

You can read more about Elijah in 1 Kings. In 2 Kings, Elijah left Elisha in charge before God sent a fiery chariot to take Elijah straight to heaven—without dying! It was an exception to the rule that every single person dies.

Elisha picked up where Elijah left off. He boldly spoke God's truth to the kings of Israel and Judah. Like Elijah, Elisha also performed miracles.

A foreign commander named Naaman suffered from a skin disease and asked Elisha for help. Elisha told him to wash in the Jordan River seven times and he'd be healed. When Naaman finally did, it worked!

Through all the miracles Elisha performed, God showed Israel and Judah that He was still right there with them. And boy, did Israel and Judah need to know that! Sin and idolatry spread from the north to the south. It infected everyone, and most of their kings just made it worse.

The northern kingdom of Israel kept rejecting God and His ways. Finally, God rejected them. He let their enemy from the north, Assyria, conquer Israel and take most of the people into captivity.

EXPECT THE UNEXPECTED

One time, Elisha helped a widow who was about to run out of food. All she had left was a bit of olive oil. Using a miracle,

Elisha multiplied the olive oil so that it filled jar after jar. Then the widow and her sons sold all that oil and made enough money to pay their bills and have a fresh start. Notice that God didn't make her super-rich. She and her sons still had to work and use their money and food responsibly. God cares about all your troubles, but His answer may not be what you ask for or expect Him to do. Trust that He will do the best thing for you anyway.

The Surviving Kingdom (2 Kings 18—25)

The kingdom of Judah lasted another 150 years. Another kingdom called Assyria tried to conquer Judah twice. But God alone is more powerful than any army. The second time they tried, God sent an angel that wiped out 185,000 Assyrian soldiers!

In the end, a different kingdom by the name of Babylon, led by King Nebuchadnezzar, invaded Judah, destroyed the temple in Jerusalem, and took the people captive.

God had finally judged Israel and Judah for disobeying Him and worshipping idols.

CULTURE SHOCK

Elisha was walking along one day, and a gang of smart-aleck kids started mouthing off to him. They told him, "Beat it, Baldy!" Elisha didn't care for that. He cursed them in the Lord's name. Then two bears charged out of the woods and attacked forty-two of the boys! You never know how having a big mouth can get you into trouble, but you can be sure it will.

Enjoy Your Trip

Where's the Gospel?

God had promised that Jesus Christ would be born from the line of David. For that to happen, at least one of David's royal descendants would have to live. At one point in 2 Kings, a woman named Athaliah decided to kill all those royal descendants! Behind the scenes, Satan was trying to stop Jesus from being born. Athaliah was selfish and mean, and Satan used that to make her do awful things. But one descendant—a boy named Joash—survived and hid away until the danger passed. David's royal line continued! God's promises can never be stopped.

PACK SMART

God saved Joash from his evil grandmother Athaliah (see 2 Kings 11). Joash became king when he was only seven years old! At first, he was a good king. He had a good advisor named Jehoiada, a priest who taught him to please God. But then Joash began to ignore God and do things his way instead of God's way. Big mistake! He owed God his life, but he ended his reign badly because he didn't want to keep trusting God.

1 AND 2 CHRONICLES

Check Your Location

A *chronicle* is a record of history. We don't know who wrote 1 and 2 Chronicles. But whoever did, they wanted to make sure the Hebrew people had a good record of their past. There's a lot of history repeated from some other books of the Bible. But there's an important difference. The other historical books are about the *political life* of Israel. These books tell about the *spiritual life* of Israel, especially the temple.

1 CHRONICLES

Plot Your Course

David's Ancestry (1 Chronicles 1–9)

The first part of 1 Chronicles is a long genealogy. A genealogy is a list of someone's ancestors. In this case, it was David's ancestors, going all the way back to Adam, the first man!

Genealogies aren't that fun to read, but they're still part of God's Word. If your name was on this list, it would be pretty cool, right? The Hebrew people, also called the Jews, used these records to keep track of whose land was whose. They also used them to keep track of who was in each tribe of Israel.

David's Activity (1 Chronicles 10–29)

The second part of 1 Chronicles tells us about the forty years

David was the king of Israel. When David was first chosen to be king, God called him "a man after his own heart" (1 Samuel 13:14). David lived to please and obey the Lord. But David also messed up a lot. He sinned and failed over and over. So why did God give David such a great compliment? The reason is simple: When David sinned, he turned back to God and asked for forgiveness.

This book tells a lot of the same stories about David included in other books of the Bible. But it mostly focuses on the good parts of David's life rather than his big "oops" moments. We get to see how God chose David because of what He saw in his heart.

And David proved himself to be a great king. A big part of 1 Chronicles tells how he made plans to build the first temple and gathered materials for it. He also gathered builders for the temple, servants who would care for it when it was finished, and worship leaders to lead the people in praising God.

A huge building project like this cost a lot of money, so David asked the Israelite people to give to it. They gave generously and from their hearts. Then they threw a party to celebrate!

In the end, David didn't get to build the temple—his son Solomon did. But David still died a happy man, "at an old age, wealthy and honored" (1 Chronicles 29:28 TLB).

David had his glory days, and he did a lot of good things. Your heavenly Father has great and important things for you to do too, just like He did for David.

PACK SMART

David had a group of loyal friends who stood by him no matter what. They were known as "David's Mighty Men." They were like an all-star team of warriors who fought God's enemies and were loyal to David. You and your friends can be heroes for God too, if you promise to follow Him no matter what and stay loyal to each other.

Enjoy Your Trip

Where's the Gospel?

What's the deal with all those lists of names in 1 Chronicles? God promised that King David would have a lineage that would last forever and ever. Jesus Christ was eventually born from the line of David and fulfilled that promise. Those names in the genealogies helped prove that Jesus was really from the line of David—that He was the true Messiah, who came just as God promised.

2 CHRONICLES

Plot Your Course

Solomon's Kingdom—Split! (2 Chronicles 1–10)

Solomon ruled Israel for forty years, leading them into a golden age. The nation expanded and got wealthier. God was with Solomon and gave him more wisdom than any other king in history!

Solomon took on two big building projects: a temple for God and a royal house for himself. God blessed Solomon with a lot of money: "Silver and gold were as plentiful in Jerusalem as rocks on the road! And expensive cedar lumber was used like common sycamore!" (2 Chronicles 1:15 TLB). When the temple was finally finished, God's glory came and filled it.

But when Solomon died, everything fell apart. Solomon's son Rehoboam was not as wise in how he ruled the people, so the people revolted, and the kingdom of Israel split in two. The northern kingdom was called Israel, and the southern kingdom was called Judah.

MUST-SEE SITES—*The Temple*

Solomon built the first temple dedicated to God (read 2 Chronicles 3). He understood that God is too big and amazing for any building to properly honor Him. But he did his best! The temple's main room was overlaid with pure gold, beautiful carvings, and jewels in the walls and doors. In the Most Holy Place, which was where God's presence would visit, the gold on the walls was nailed into place with gold nails! Solomon tried his hardest to honor God, and the result was a magnificent building where people could offer worship and sacrifices to the Lord.

The Southern Kingdom Goes South (2 Chronicles 11–36)

The rest of 2 Chronicles focuses on the kings of Judah. It only mentions a few of the kings of Israel. Most of the kings of Judah after Solomon did evil things. They disobeyed God, and they worshipped idols. Sounds familiar, doesn't it?

But instead of focusing on all the bad kings, I want to point out one of the very best kings Judah had during this time. His name was Josiah.

Josiah became king at *eight years old*! Yet he was Judah's godliest leader. While he was young, he got to know God for himself. As he grew up, Josiah got rid of all the idols in the land. When he was twenty-six, he fixed up the temple and made it look nice again. While that was happening, one of the priests found a copy of the Law—the first five books of the Bible. It had been forgotten for years!

When Josiah read it, he was heartbroken over his nation's sin. So he gathered all the people and read it to them. They were heartbroken too. Then everyone promised to follow God's rules.

But after Josiah, it was all downhill. The people stopped

following the Lord even after God gave them lots of chances to follow Him again. So finally the Lord let the kingdom of Babylon attack Judah. Babylon destroyed Jerusalem and the temple, and then they took the people as prisoners.

TOUR GUIDE

- I became king when I was sixteen.
- I honored God by fighting His enemies and feeding His people.
- My life went downhill when I got a big head about the success God gave me. He had to set me straight by giving me a nasty disease called leprosy.
- Read 2 Chronicles 26:3-5,16-21 to see who I am.

Enjoy Your Trip

Where's the Gospel?

Did you know that Jesus talked about His body as if it was a temple? (Look up Matthew 12:6.) The temple Solomon built was a way God could be near His people. But Jesus was God Himself. That means that through Jesus, God could also be near His people, but in person!

EZRA

Check Your Location

Ezra was the name of a Jewish priest and scribe (someone who writes important documents). The book of Ezra is nicknamed the Second Exodus. The Israelites, now called Jews, had lived as slaves in Babylon for seventy years. Finally, they got to return to the Promised Land. It was like what happened when Moses delivered them from Egypt centuries earlier. This time, they returned three different times in three different groups. Their leaders were Zerubbabel, Ezra, and Nehemiah. Ezra, who wrote this book, talked about the first two times.

Plot Your Course

The Nation Returns (Ezra 1–6)

The Jews had been captives in Babylon for seventy years. Then Persia conquered Babylon. That meant that the Jews were still living in Babylon, but Babylon was under Persian control. The king of Persia at that time was named Cyrus. God inspired Cyrus to let the Jews return to their home and rebuild the destroyed temple.

A man named Zerubbabel led 49,987 Jews back to Israel. That sounds like a lot of people, but about a million Jews stayed behind in Babylon. They had become comfortable even though they weren't free. They didn't want to go back home![1]

---

[1] Rabbi Ken Spiro, "History Crash Course #43: The Jews of Babylon," Aish.com, http://www.aish.com/jl/h/cc/48949881.html.

The smaller group of Jews returned to Israel. Once they were back, the first thing Zerubbabel and the Jews did was start making the animal sacrifices. That was because God required them to in His Law. They wanted to make sure they were obeying the Lord. Then they laid the foundation for the temple and threw a big party.

But soon, an enemy showed up. The people who had been living in the land this whole time said they wanted to help rebuild the temple. But Zerubbabel didn't let them. This was a project for God's people, the Jews. So these enemies got angry and got the Persian king to command the Jews to stop rebuilding the temple.

For sixteen years, the work stopped. The Jews became discouraged. Then God sent two prophets to snap them back into action. With the king's permission to keep building, the Jews finished the temple a few years later. They dedicated it with a big celebration!

LEARN THE LANGUAGE—*Encourage*

Ezra said that God "encouraged" him by making the king of Persia and his royal advisors like him and support his cause (Ezra 7:28). To encourage means to strengthen someone's heart so they feel like they can overcome a hard time. When you say nice things to people and boost their spirits, you are an encourager. We all need to encourage and be encouraged by others.

The Nation Is Revived (Ezra 7–10)

Almost sixty years went by. Then Ezra came to Jerusalem with more Jews from Babylon.

Ezra, a priest and a scribe, came to reteach the law of God to the people. A scribe wrote down copies of the Bible by hand, so Ezra was the perfect choice to teach the people. Most of the Jews in Jerusalem had disobeyed God by marrying *pagans*. Pagans were local people who didn't believe in God. Ezra was so upset, he tore his clothes and ripped out some of his hair as a way to show his sadness over their sin. *Ouch!*

Ezra prayed to the Lord and confessed the people's sins. Many of the Jews joined him. Then Ezra challenged them to separate from their pagan spouses. It took a few months, but God used Ezra to help get the nation back in line with His commandments.

Why should you and I care about the Jews moving back into the Promised Land? Because the Bible tells us that Israel is the center of history. God's plans are focused on the Jewish nation because Jesus would eventually be born there. What happens in Israel affects everyone else all over the world. God had promised the Jews that He would bring them back to the land after their captivity. In Ezra, we see that God always keeps His promises.

Enjoy Your Trip

God's Words Are Powerful!

God sent the prophets Haggai and Zechariah to encourage the people to keep rebuilding the temple when it got hard. They shared God's words and inspired the people to keep working. When do you listen to God's words? Do you hear them at church? Do you read the Bible on your own? God's words are powerful to help you in your life.

The Lord Keeps Working on You

It took a long time for the temple in Jerusalem to finally be rebuilt. But God kept working on it, using His people. Sometimes it feels like God takes a long time to work in our lives. But He never gives up on us, even when things are hard. Philippians

1:6 says, "God who began the good work within you will keep right on helping you grow in his grace until his task within you is finally finished" (TLB). God never gives up on you!

Where's the Gospel?

Where do we see Jesus Christ in the book of Ezra? Zerubbabel was a descendant of the royal line of David. This meant he was an ancestor of Jesus. When Ezra told the Jews to separate from the pagan spouses, he was actually preparing for the Messiah. He was making sure that the royal line of Jesus stayed pure according to God's standards.

NEHEMIAH

Check Your Location

The book of Nehemiah tells the story of how the Jews returned to Jerusalem and rebuilt the walls around the city. About fourteen years after Ezra and the people rebuilt the temple, a man named Nehemiah and a final group of Jews came to Jerusalem to help strengthen the broken-down city. But rebuilding was harder than they thought it would be. If a construction project doesn't sound that exciting to you, how about swords and schemes?

Plot Your Course

Building the Wall (Nehemiah 1—7)

Nehemiah had been working as a cupbearer to the king of Persia while Israel was imprisoned there. Then he heard about the Jews who had gone back to Jerusalem. It wasn't a good report: The city had no protection from its enemies.

Nehemiah was very sad about his homeland. So he talked to God about the situation. The king noticed Nehemiah was upset and asked him about it. Nehemiah told the king about Jerusalem and asked for permission to help rebuild the city. And the king gave it!

So Nehemiah traveled back home to Jerusalem. Soon he and the Jews began building a wall around the city. But this got the attention of some local officials who didn't like the Jews. These enemies started making fun of them and threatening them. Nehemiah told them to get lost—God was helping them, so they weren't going to give up.

But when the Jews built the wall to half its height, one of these officials met with the local army and made plans to attack the Jews. The Jews were afraid and discouraged. But Nehemiah prayed and then came up with a plan. Everyone worked on the wall with a building tool in one hand and a weapon in the other. They weren't going to stop working, and they were prepared to defend themselves!

Nehemiah and the Jews faced many other hardships. But Nehemiah stayed true to God and kept working on the wall. The wall was finished in record time: fifty-two days! It was something only God could have made happen.

EXPECT THE UNEXPECTED

A cupbearer sounds like the guy who brings the king his royal lemonade, but he was actually the king's right-hand man. Nehemiah did all kinds of hard jobs for the king—including taking the first sip from the king's cup to make sure it wasn't poisoned! Because he did such a good job, God made sure the king wanted to help Nehemiah when he asked the king if he could go to Jerusalem. Anything you do for God is worth doing well. God can do incredible things when you do your best for Him.

PACK SMART

Nehemiah was smart in how he dealt with bullies. He didn't quit because of them. He told the king and prepared his friends to stick together and defend themselves. Even more important, he prayed and trusted God to help him. Remember, Jesus loves everyone and wants everyone to get along. Seek help, protect yourself, stand up for the helpless, and be ready to forgive, just as God forgives you.

Kick-Starting a Revival (Nehemiah 8—10)

After the walls of Jerusalem were finished, Ezra the priest read the Bible to all the people. The people wept when they heard how far they had fallen away from God. But Nehemiah reminded them that first it was time for celebrating the completion of the wall.

Later, they grieved over their sin. They confessed how they had messed up, and they worshipped God. Then Ezra prayed the longest prayer ever recorded in the Bible. When he was done, the people made a promise to follow God's Law. Israel turned back to God once again. It was a huge revival!

Dealing with the People (Nehemiah 11—13)

There was one problem: Jerusalem was a ghost town. Not many Jews had returned to Jerusalem over the years. Many of them lived outside the city walls. So Nehemiah told one-tenth of the people to come live in the city.

When that was taken care of, it was finally party time. That day, "the joy of the people of Jerusalem was heard far away!" (Nehemiah 12:43 TLB).

Nehemiah still had to take care of some problems. But he did this head-on, knowing that God would help him.

Enjoy Your Trip

We All Get to Work on the Wall

In Nehemiah, forty-two different groups and thirty-eight

people helped build the wall. Imagine having your name in the Bible as someone who helped God! It also tells us that Nehemiah couldn't do it all by himself. It's the same with God's people, the church. We all need to get along and work together to serve God. Don't be a loner. Find a friend and serve God together.

Where's the Gospel?

Jerusalem is a special city to God. Psalm 87:2 calls Jerusalem "the city of God, the city he loves more than any other!" (TLB). Why? Because Jerusalem is the center of salvation. Jesus died on a cross right outside the city walls, making it possible for anyone to be saved from their sin.

▶ Nehemiah Rebuilds Jerusalem's Walls

Read about the builder-warriors in Nehemiah 4:15-18.

ESTHER

Check Your Location

The book of Esther is like a fairy tale and mystery story combined—only it really happened! It took place in Persia while some of the Jews were returning to Jerusalem after their captivity. Brave and beautiful Esther became the queen of Persia, where many exiled Jews still lived. But then the villain Haman plotted to destroy her people, the Jews. Would she and her cousin, the hero Mordecai, be able to save the Jews before it was too late?

Plot Your Course

The Beauty Contest (Esther 1–2)

Judah, Israel's southern kingdom, was conquered by Babylon, but then Babylon was conquered by Persia. Ahasuerus became the new king. After he kicked his old queen off the throne, he rounded up the most beautiful girls in the land so he could choose a new queen.

A Jewish man named Mordecai entered his young cousin Esther into the beauty contest. Esther blew the king away with her looks and gentle spirit. Just like that, he crowned her the new queen. But Mordecai told Esther to keep her heritage—that she was a Jew—a secret.

Then Mordecai got a job at the royal palace. One day, he heard about a plot to kill the king, so he told Esther, who told the king, and the plot was stopped.

The Bad Guy (Esther 3—5)

But another bad guy lurked in the shadows: Haman. Haman was an important guy in the king's court. The king told everyone to bow down before Haman, but Mordecai wouldn't.

Haman hated Mordecai for not kissing up to him. Then Haman found out Mordecai was a Jew and decided to have all the Jews in Persia killed. Haman even tricked the king into giving him permission to carry out his plan.

Mordecai heard the news and told Esther. Esther was scared that if she showed up before the king without being invited (which was against the law), she could be put to death. But Mordecai told Esther that maybe she had become queen for this very reason: to speak up and save the Jews from Haman's threat.

So Esther went before the king. But she only asked for permission to throw a dinner party for the king and Haman. At the party, the king told Esther to ask for whatever she wanted. She only asked the two men to come to another party the next night.

In the meantime, Haman built a gallows seventy-five feet tall that he planned on using to kill Mordecai. His plan was going to happen!

A Blessed Ending (Esther 6—10)

But God made sure that things went badly for Haman at Esther's second party. Esther finally got the courage to tell the king about Haman's plot and asked him to save the lives of her people. King Ahasuerus was furious when he found out, so he had Haman arrested and hanged on the same gallows Haman made for Mordecai!

In the end, the Jewish people were saved, and Mordecai got Haman's job. Jews everywhere threw a huge feast, and many Persian people even chose to believe in God because of this miracle. The day became an official holiday that the Jews still celebrate: the feast of Purim.

Even while the Jewish people lived in exile in Persia, God didn't forget about them—He continued to protect them and deliver them from their enemies. God is always faithful!

EXPECT THE UNEXPECTED

There's no mention of God in the book of Esther. But He's still there! He made sure Esther was in the right place at the right time so that she would be able to save God's people, the Jews. Even when it doesn't seem like God is with you, He always is.

Enjoy Your Trip

Inner Beauty

Esther caught the king's eye with her outward beauty, but she won his heart with her character—who she was on the inside. When you spend regular time with God, He builds His character in you. Because of that, you love Him more and want to do the right thing to honor Him. That character is more important than any physical beauty. It will definitely last longer!

Where's the Gospel?

It's easy to see that Satan inspired Haman's plot against the Jews. But God had promised that the Savior, Jesus Christ, would be born into the Jewish nation. If Haman killed all the Jews, it could stop Jesus from being born. God's plans can never be stopped—*ever!*

CULTURE SHOCK

Part of the Jewish celebration of Purim—the story of Esther—is eating triangle-shaped cookies called *hamantaschen*.

That means "Haman's ears." It probably refers to the Persian practice of cutting off a criminal's ears before he was executed. As gross as that sounds, it's a pretty normal way for Jews to remember their history: "They tried to kill us, God saved us, let's eat cookies!"

JOB

Check Your Location

We're not sure who wrote the book of Job or when. But a lot of scholars think this is the oldest book in the Bible. This book tells the story of a man named Job (pronounced "Jobe") and the worst time in his life. God let Satan kill Job's kids, destroy Job's property, shrink his riches, and give Job a nasty disease. Yeah, it's depressing! But don't skip this one. You might just find out the answer to Job's biggest question: Why does God let us go through bad times?

Plot Your Course

Job's Suffering (Job 1—2)

God blessed Job with ten children, thousands of animals, and a bunch of servants. And Job honored God and made sacrifices to Him on behalf of his whole family. God even called Job "the finest man in all the earth" (Job 1:8).

But Satan came before God and said, "Hey, Job only respects You because You've given him everything he could ever want. Take it away and see what happens." So God gave Satan permission to ruin Job's life. Job's animals were stolen, his servants were killed, and a tornado killed all of his kids!

How did Job respond? He worshipped God! He was sad, but he didn't get mad at God or blame Him. Satan was still hostile toward Job. He told God, "He only worships You because he still has good health." So God let Satan give Job a gross disease. But Job still didn't sin against God even though he was in horrible pain. Job loved God more than all the good stuff God had given him.

CULTURE SHOCK

Scholars and doctors aren't sure what Job's disease was. All we know for sure is that it was painful and disgusting. His body was covered with infected boils—sort of like evil acne. They itched and burned, and when he scratched at them, they got worse. Maggots grew in the wounds, and pus oozed everywhere. Even though Job wished the disease would just get it over with and kill him, he still didn't give up on God.

Job's Sidekicks (Job 3—37)

Job's three friends—Eliphaz, Bildad, and Zophar—soon showed up. They wanted to comfort Job. They did at first by quietly sitting with him and just listening to him. But they should have kept their mouths shut!

The three guys spoke up and basically said the same thing over and over again: "Job, God is punishing you for something bad you've done." They believed that if you're really godly, you'll never go through tough times. But that isn't true! After these three not-so-friendly friends gave their speeches, a younger guy named Elihu spoke up. He had a whole different take on Job's suffering, but it didn't help Job out much at all. He needed to hear from God!

EXPECT THE UNEXPECTED

Satan is not in hell—not yet, at least. He will be at the end of time, but in the meantime, he still has access to earth. Sometimes he can even go to God's throne room in heaven! In Job, God asked Satan where he had been. Satan said, "Hanging out on earth, going all over the place." Don't freak out, though! God has Satan on a leash. The devil only does what God allows him to. And God only allows him to test us so that we will learn to trust God more. God won't let your suffering last forever. He won't let Satan stick you in the oven while He goes on vacation and leaves you baking.

Job's Success (Job 38–42)

Finally, God stepped in and spoke to Job from the middle of a huge storm. God explained how He made the universe (and that Job didn't!) and He is in control of everything, including the bad times. God didn't explain why He let Satan attack Job. He just reminded Job of His power and might. Job understood that God worked in ways he didn't understand but that God was still God.

So Job humbled himself before God. That means he recognized he was small and God is big. Job didn't understand why he was suffering, but he knew God did. So Job trusted God.

When Job's suffering ended, the Lord blessed him even more than He had before! Job had ten more kids and twice as much wealth. He lived a good life for the rest of his days.

Am I glad we have the book of Job! It shows us that God can make good things come out of bad things even when all we see are the bad things. When we can't see the good, we can trust that God is still at work.

PACK SMART

There are two worlds that exist side by side: the physical world and the spiritual world. The spiritual world is invisible, but it's just as important as the world we can see—*and just as real*. We know that Satan did all this to Job. But Job didn't know this. He couldn't see it happening. However, God ultimately controls both worlds, so it's important to trust Him with what you can *and* can't see.

Enjoy Your Trip

How to Deal with the Bad Stuff

Have you ever gone through a hard time? How did you feel toward God? God sometimes lets bad things happen to you even when you don't understand why. But this is what Job learned: You don't trust God because He makes your life easy or gives you lots of good things. You trust Him because He is always in control and will always do what's best for you. God can make good things come out of bad things (see Romans 8:28). In fact, it's His specialty!

Where's the Gospel?

Suffering is very real. But not everything that hurts is bad. Think of Jesus: He was beaten and killed to pay the price for your sins—which is a very good thing! Job understood that. He believed that God was going to send a Messiah (or Redeemer) to save the world. He said, "I know that my Redeemer lives, and that he will stand upon the earth at last" (Job 19:25 TLB). Job predicted Jesus Christ was coming!

PSALMS

Check Your Location

If you like music and the lyrics to songs, then Psalms is the book for you. (And even if you don't, Psalms is still awesome!) Psalms used to be the songbook Israel used for their worship services. A psalm is a song or poem written about God or written to God. King David wrote most of the psalms. He was a skilled musician. They express almost every feeling you can think of: joy, sadness, fear, thankfulness, and many more. They also talk about a lot of different topics, including God's power and love.

Plot Your Course

The book of Psalms is divided into five sections. Let's look at one or two psalms from each section and learn something about God.

Section One (Psalms 1—41)

In Psalm 19, David told us how God speaks through the wonders of His creation. If nature is beautiful, how much more beautiful the Artist must be! God also speaks through His Word, the Bible. This is how He can tell us specific things about Himself—like how much He loves us.

Psalm 23 is probably the most famous psalm. It talks about what it means to live under the care of God, the Great Shepherd. A loving shepherd like the Lord keeps His sheep happy, well fed, and safe from danger.

LEARN THE LANGUAGE—*Hope*

When David wrote, "For in You, O Lord, I hope" (Psalm 38:15 NKJV), the Hebrew word he used for "hope" also means "wait." David waited for God to help him. Because God is strong and because He cares about you, you can be confident that He will help you when the time is right.

Section Two (Psalms 42–72)

In Psalms 32 and 51, David talked about how good it is to confess your sin to God. It can be hard, but it's better to ask God for forgiveness. It's too stressful to keep your sin a secret!

Section Three (Psalms 73–89)

The sons of Korah, who wrote Psalm 84, were a family who led worship in the temple. They wrote, "I would rather be a gatekeeper in the house of my God than live the good life in the homes of the wicked" (verse 10). It wasn't glamorous to be a gatekeeper. They had to open the doors and keep track of who was going in and out of the temple. But anything you do to make God look good (instead of yourself) shows a humble attitude that God loves.

Section Four (Psalms 90–106)

Psalm 90 is the only psalm that Moses wrote. He prayed, "Teach us to number our days and recognize how few they are; help us to spend them as we should" (verse 12 TLB). There are some things you have to spend your time doing, like school, chores, and homework. But you can choose how you spend your free time. Ask God to help you make all that time count for good.

Section Five (Psalms 107–150)

Psalm 119 is the longest chapter in the Bible. And it's *all* about the Bible! This psalm shows that the Bible helps us every day, in every part of our lives.

In Psalm 139, David wrote about God's qualities:

- God knows everything about everything and everyone.
- God is everywhere, all the time.
- God is almighty. He made all the galaxies—and He also made you!
- God cares about you.

Psalm 150, the final psalm, tells us to praise God. He's worthy of it! Even if you can't play an instrument or sing very well, you should still praise Him. God is the reason you have life and a purpose for your life.

CULTURE SHOCK

Some psalms ask God to deal with enemies in a harsh way. (For examples, check out Psalms 10, 35, 58, and 59.) That sounds odd for a worship song, doesn't it? Besides, Jesus told us to love our enemies and pray for them.

But here's the thing: The Israelites were under constant attack. The surrounding nations often wanted to get rid of the Jews permanently. So God's people would cry out to Him in these psalms, begging Him to deal with those who were trying to destroy them.

We can be honest with God about our true feelings even though He doesn't have to answer those prayers. These psalms can also teach us how to feel what other people feel, especially when they are hurting.

Enjoy Your Trip

Like a Tree

Psalm 1 says if you love reading and thinking about the Bible, you'll be like a strong tree planted by a river. A tree like that provides shade and produces lots of fruit. A good life is like that. Nothing can uproot you because God is your strength. You have good relationships and do lots of helpful things. But if you don't follow God, you'll have a bad life with a bad ending. This is why I want you to understand and love the Bible.

Be Honest!

The Psalms show us that when you talk to God, you should be honest. God knows everything anyway, so you can never fool Him. And He can handle your feelings. So tell Him the things you can't tell anyone else. Then depend on Him to help you every day.

Where's the Gospel?

Some of the psalms predict different things about Jesus Christ. For example, Psalm 2 talks about how nothing—not even all the world's leaders—can stand up against God and "his anointed" (verse 2). Another word we use for "God's Anointed" is *Messiah*. In other words, this is talking about the Messiah, Jesus Christ. Nothing and no one can stop Jesus.

Psalm 22 is another psalm about Jesus. In fact, when Jesus died on the cross, He quoted verse 1: "My God, my God, why have you abandoned me?" (look up Matthew 27:46 and Mark 15:34). The rest of Psalm 22 describes all the suffering Jesus would go through on the cross—hundreds of years before it even happened!

PROVERBS, ECCLESIASTES, AND SONG OF SOLOMON

Check Your Location

The Bible calls King Solomon the wisest man of his time (see 1 Kings 4:30). He wrote down a lot of his wisdom, which we have in the books of Proverbs, Ecclesiastes, and Song of Solomon.

Proverbs is the best how-to book ever written. It tells us how to live good lives and be happy. A proverb is a short, wise saying about life. These proverbs were inspired by God. That means they're not just *good* advice—they're *God's* advice!

In Ecclesiastes, Solomon looked back on his life. He was older and wanted to answer an important question: "What's the purpose of my life?" Ecclesiastes was sort of like his personal journal to figure out what life was all about.

The Song of Solomon was written by King Solomon when he was a young man. He wrote 1,005 songs, but this was his best love song. It tells the story of how Solomon met and married a country girl.

PROVERBS

Plot Your Course

Proverbs has a lot of topics. I'm going to focus on four big ones that pop up throughout the book.

Respect God

Proverbs 1:7 says, "Fear of the LORD is the foundation of true knowledge." Fearing the Lord doesn't mean you're scared that God is going to hit you with a bolt of lightning when you mess up. Fearing God means you respect and admire Him, so you want to obey Him. It's like when you obey your parents because you don't want to disappoint them.

Fearing the Lord will make life so much better! Instead of being worried about what other people think about you, you live to make God happy. Life is better that way.

Don't Be Lazy!

Proverbs tells us to be diligent in everything we do. To be diligent means to work hard and do our best. This means we're not supposed to sit around all day doing nothing (see Proverbs 6:6-11). There's no excuse for a Christian to be lazy, whether at home or at school.

Words Are Powerful

We need to be careful about what we say: "The tongue can bring death or life" (Proverbs 18:21). Our words have the power to build others up or tear them down.

Sometimes it's hard to control what you say to other people. But God hates it when you lie, gossip, and say mean things. So the solution is to do what God loves: Choose your words carefully. Be honest. Be kind. Guarding your tongue is a very wise thing to do!

Get Good Friends

Having friends (and I don't just mean "friends" or followers on social media!) is one of the best things about life. A true friend "is always loyal" (Proverbs 17:17). A true friend also helps you be the best you can be: "As iron sharpens iron, so a friend sharpens a friend" (Proverbs 27:17).

But remember that to have a friend, you need to be friendly yourself! Even if you're shy, just try being friendly to someone else. It shows people that you care. It might be easier than you think to make a new friend.

LEARN THE LANGUAGE—*Wisdom*

"Tune your ears to wisdom, and concentrate on understanding" (Proverbs 2:2). Wisdom isn't the same thing as intelligence. Some people are really smart in school but not so smart in life. The Bible says being wise is learning what God says to do and then doing it. Not to do so is to be a fool. There are a lot of smart people who act foolishly.

Enjoy Your Trip

Don't Just Listen—Do!

Solomon said lots of wise things, and early in his reign as king, he did a lot of wise things too. But as time went on, he stopped actually following and obeying the Lord. That was unwise, and it led to Solomon making some really bad decisions. Reading and studying the Bible doesn't mean anything unless you do what it tells you to do. Try choosing one proverb to memorize. Here are a few to consider: Proverbs 1:7; 3:5-6; 4:23; 15:1; and 18:24. How will it change the way you act today?

Where's the Gospel?

Proverbs tells you how to live wisely. But you can't do this all alone—you need Jesus to help. The Bible says that only in Jesus can you find "all the treasures of wisdom and knowledge"

(Colossians 2:3). That means that Jesus will give you the wisdom and strength to live right before God.

ECCLESIASTES

Plot Your Course

Solomon's Search (Ecclesiastes 1—10)

Solomon started his book on a depressing note: Everything is vanity, or *emptiness*. *Vanity* means *breath*. Solomon was saying that everything is here one minute and gone the next, like a breath. In the end, it's meaningless.

How could he say something like that? He had experienced every good thing in life: riches, power, pleasure, food and drink, marriage (*lots* of marriages!). But none of it satisfied him. So he asked, "What's the point of living?"

Yikes! That sounds pretty hopeless, doesn't it? But Solomon actually discovered something that all of us need to learn. Without God, nothing in this world can make you happy for very long. You'll always want something more. That's because you weren't made to be satisfied with anything in this world.

That new video game will be fun for a while. The coolest clothes will be cool until the next trend. And trying to be popular is like swimming with sharks. Nothing this world has to offer will ever truly make you happy. Only God can. That's why He put a hole in your soul—the inner, eternal part of you—that only He can fill.

Solomon wrote down a bunch of sayings that basically said this same thing. The big idea was still *vanity*—everything except God is useless.

Having lots of money won't help much, Solomon said. Owning more things can't fill up your soul. And sometimes, bad things happen to good people and good things happen to bad people! Life is unfair. What's the point of it all?

Solomon's Solution (Ecclesiastes 11—12)

Finally, Solomon brought God into the picture as he looked for something to fill the God-sized hole in his soul. Makes sense! He had some advice specifically for you: "Don't let the excitement of being young cause you to forget about your Creator" (Ecclesiastes 12:1 TLB). It's good to enjoy life while you're young, but don't forget about the Lord! He's the only one who can give you a purpose for living. That's what Solomon found out in the end.

Enjoy Your Trip

Where's the Gospel?

Solomon found out that life "under the sun" (meaning life on this earth) doesn't have any lasting purpose. But we know that life under the *Son of God*, Jesus Christ, is very different! With Jesus, life is full of meaning. Jesus said, "My purpose is to give [you] a rich and satisfying life" (John 10:10).

SONG OF SOLOMON

Plot Your Course

The Engagement (Song of Solomon 1:1—3:5)

When Solomon was young, he met a beautiful girl, and they fell in love. This book calls her the Shulamite (she was from a village called Shulem).

Solomon and the Shulamite got engaged. In the olden days, couples spent lots of time together so they could know each other's character better. This couple grew closer and closer.

But they also wanted to stay pure before marriage. That's why the Shulamite told her friends, "Promise me...not to awaken love until the time is right" (Song of Solomon 2:7).

God's plan is that only a married man and woman can experience sexual love. God Himself invented sex! But that means only He gets to tell us when it's okay. Sex is a good thing in the right place. It's like fire: It's good in a fireplace but not on the carpet! Marriage is the only safe place for sexual love. So Solomon and the Shulamite did things God's way and waited until they were married.

The Wedding (Song of Solomon 3:6—5:1)

Finally, they got to celebrate their wedding. Afterward, they were free to enjoy sexual love as husband and wife. They did things the right way, so God blessed them. God loves to bless people who obey Him.

The Marriage (Song of Solomon 5:2—8:14)

In the last few chapters of this book, Solomon and the Shulamite's marriage grew stronger. They had an argument, but then they worked out their problem. That led to an even better relationship than they had before!

This love song Solomon wrote points to God's love for us. His love is better than any romantic love we could ever experience. God pursues you and will never give up on you or abandon you. He will always try to help you in the best way possible.

PACK SMART

The Shulamite worried about how she looked. "Don't stare at me because I am dark—the sun has darkened my skin," she said (Song of Solomon 1:6). In those days, pale skin was considered more beautiful than tanned skin. But Solomon didn't care. He loved her just the way she was.

Today, there are lots of messages on social media or television that tell you that you don't have the right looks. Be careful! It's okay to care about your looks as long as you don't become obsessed with them. Don't put yourself down or harm yourself in order to appear better looking.

Enjoy Your Trip

Character over Cuteness

You're not going to get married anytime soon! But when you do start looking for a husband or wife, put character first. *Character* is who someone is on the inside. It's okay to think someone is cute, but Solomon's wife liked his character more than anything else.

Where's the Gospel?

Although Song of Solomon tells a true love story between a husband and wife, it also points to the love Jesus has for you and me. Jesus loves us so much He died for us on the cross! In fact, a married couple's love is supposed to be a way of seeing how much Jesus and His followers love each other (see Ephesians 5:31-32).

ISAIAH

Check Your Location

Isaiah is the first big book of prophecy in the Bible. Prophecy is when God predicts what's going to happen in the future, usually through a person called a prophet, like Isaiah. Isaiah spoke God's messages to Judah, the southern kingdom of the Jews, for about fifty years. Isaiah said that because of the people's sin, God was going to let their enemy defeat them. It would be like a nationwide time-out for seventy years. (We read about that back in the chapters about Israel's kings.) But Isaiah also said that after God judged Judah, He would heal and restore them.

Plot Your Course

Prophecies About God's Judgment (Isaiah 1–39)

When Isaiah became God's prophet, the neighboring nation of Assyria had already conquered the northern kingdom of Israel. So Assyria turned its attention toward Judah, the southern kingdom.

God told Isaiah that He was going to let one of their biggest enemies come and take them captive. Why? Because the people had rebelled against Him, so He was going to judge their sin.

But Isaiah also promised that hope was coming. He looked far into the future and saw that God was one day going to deliver the entire world from its biggest enemy, sin, through the Messiah. We know who this Messiah turned out to be: Jesus Christ.

Isaiah also prophesied about the nine different nations God was going to use to punish Judah. Isaiah warned his people about this punishment. He tried to stop them from living a sinful life. He knew destruction was coming if they didn't stop!

Prophecies About God's Comfort (Isaiah 40—66)

Like a parent, God sometimes punishes His people for their wrongdoing first and then comforts them afterward. That was the case with Judah. First, they were going to be taken captive by their enemy—not Assyria, but another kingdom called Babylon. Then one day, God was going to bring them back home.

Far in the future, God would comfort them—and you and me—by sending the Messiah. Isaiah had some of the clearest prophecies about who the Messiah would be and what He would do. Most important, Isaiah predicted how the Messiah would save people from the biggest enemy of all: their own sin.

Isaiah also predicted how God would protect the people of Israel until the end of the world. During the end times, Jesus will come back and take over as the King of the world. He will bring peace to the earth for 1,000 years, and then He will defeat Satan for good and make a whole new world for us to live in forever. And Isaiah foretold it all. What a prophet!

EXPECT THE UNEXPECTED

It's hard to imagine a world where people don't get sick or hurt or divorced or depressed. But that's what will happen during the 1,000 years Jesus will reign on earth (read Isaiah 11:6-12). Jesus will make everything right. There will be no broken homes, no broken hearts, no diseases, no hospitals, no funerals, and no sadness. Can you imagine that?

TOUR GUIDE

- My name in Hebrew means "shining one" or "day star."
- I served God but then decided I wanted His job.
- Jesus watched me fall from heaven.
- Read Isaiah 14:12-14 and Luke 10:18 to find out who I am.

Enjoy Your Trip

Perfect Prophecy Record

Prophecy is one thing that makes God unique. Only God has a perfect record when it comes to predicting the future. Many of the things God predicted through the prophets have already occurred. That means that when the Lord says something will happen, it's going to happen.

Where's the Gospel?

Isaiah talked a lot about the Messiah, who we know is Jesus Christ. He said that Jesus would be God's perfect Servant. On the cross, Jesus took our place and paid the price of our sin before God. That's what God sent Jesus to do, and Jesus served God faithfully. As Isaiah said, "He was wounded and bruised for *our* sins. He was beaten that we might have peace; he was lashed—and we were healed!...God laid on *him* the guilt and sins of every one of us!" (Isaiah 53:5-6 TLB).

LEARN THE LANGUAGE—*Forever*

Isaiah said, "The grass withers and the flowers fade, but the word of our God stands forever" (Isaiah 40:8). *Forever* is a long time! Nothing in the universe will last as long as God's Word, the Bible. So don't let your Bible sit on the shelf and collect dust. Read it and live it out. It will bring peace and joy to your life.

JEREMIAH

Check Your Location

The prophet Jeremiah wrote this book during the last years of Judah, the southern kingdom of the Jews. Jeremiah had a hard job. He had to tell God's people that God was going to let their enemy, Babylon, come and take them captive. No one really believed Jeremiah. But Babylon eventually did come to attack them. The Babylonians destroyed the city of Jerusalem and took the people as their slaves. Even so, Jeremiah gave the people hope.

Plot Your Course

Jeremiah's Predictions (Jeremiah 1–51)

God called Jeremiah to be His prophet when Jeremiah was just a young man. God told Jeremiah that speaking His truth to the people of Judah was going to be hard. And it was! After forty years of preaching, Jeremiah didn't see a single person turn back to the Lord. Can you imagine how hard that would be?

But Jeremiah still said what God wanted him to say. Through Jeremiah, God told the people to leave their sin and come back to serving Him. Then God would forgive them and bring them back from Babylon.

But there were many false prophets who lied about what the Lord said. They made the people think everything was all right, so the people stopped listening to Jeremiah. Jeremiah was heartbroken. He wept because he knew what was going to happen if they didn't start following the Lord again.

The people got annoyed with Jeremiah's talk of doom and destruction, so they beat him up and threw him in jail. He almost quit serving God—but he couldn't. The words God told him to speak were like a fire inside him! He had to let them out.

So Jeremiah got back to work. He kept telling the people of Judah that they were going to be taken captive by Babylon. But there was a tiny sliver of hope. After seventy years of captivity, God was going to free the people and bring them back to their homeland. Then Jeremiah saw that, far in the future, God would send His Messiah to save the people from their sin.

But for the moment, God's judgment was a done deal. Babylon attacked Judah three different times and took most of the people as slaves to Babylon, but God kept speaking through Jeremiah.

EXPECT THE UNEXPECTED

Babylon was the mightiest empire in the world when it conquered Judah. It was world-famous for its military power, its great kings, and its beautiful buildings, gardens, streets, and walls. But God was using Babylon to teach His people a lesson. All the human power in the world is nothing compared to God's might. God can use whoever He wants to accomplish His plans.

Jeremiah's Predictions Come True (Jeremiah 52)

The last chapter of this book talks about how all of Jeremiah's prophecies came true. Things were horrible for the people of Judah! But here's the hope that Jeremiah gave them: One day, God was going to help them and bring them back home.

PACK SMART

Jeremiah's life reminds us that we need to tell others what God says in His Word, the Bible—no matter how hard it is. In fact, we should expect it to be hard. Many people don't like to hear about God's truth, but when you rely on God for help, you can do anything He tells you to do! So stand up for the truth. God has got your back.

Enjoy Your Trip

Before You Were Born

When God called Jeremiah to be a prophet, He told Jeremiah that He had planned his life before he was even born! God knows each of us way before we're growing in our mothers. He has good plans for each of us. That means we can trust Him to take care of everything we need.

Where's the Gospel?

Jesus was a lot like Jeremiah. He told people the truth even when they didn't want to hear it. His heart broke over sin. He even wept over the city of Jerusalem. But He also knew that God would make things right again. Through Jesus, God made it so that we could escape judgment for our sin.

LAMENTATIONS

Check Your Location

Just as God predicted, Babylon came along and attacked Judah, the southern kingdom. Its soldiers set fire to the city of Jerusalem. They also took a lot of people as their prisoners. The prophet Jeremiah probably wrote Lamentations shortly after all this happened. Lamentations is a collection of sad poems about the destruction he saw.

Plot Your Course

Sad Songs for God (Lamentations 1—5)

A lamentation is a song or poem about grief, the sadness you feel when someone dies. Jeremiah had every reason to be sad. He watched Jerusalem and Judah be conquered by Babylon. He knew this was going to happen, but it was still horrible to see!

Jeremiah wrote about how the city of Jerusalem was left all alone, with no one to help. Many of the people were killed by the Babylonian soldiers or starved to death. All their wealth was stolen.

And God was the one who allowed this to happen! It wasn't that He was in a bad mood or liked to watch His people suffer. Judah had messed up. They disobeyed and ran away from the Lord for such a long time, so He was giving them a serious time-out. It was the only way to snap them out of their sin and get them to start following Him again.

During this horrible time, Jeremiah didn't give up. Instead, he thought of the promises God made. That's how he could say this: "There is one ray of hope: his compassion never ends. It is only the Lord's mercies that have kept us from complete destruction. Great is his faithfulness; his loving-kindness begins afresh each day" (Lamentations 3:21-23 TLB).

Jeremiah knew that God loves people and is in control of our lives, and he trusted that God was going to make things right again one day. That gave him hope even when everything around him seemed like it was falling apart. Jeremiah ended this book by asking God to keep His promises and not forget about His people.

LEARN THE LANGUAGE—*Faithful*

Jeremiah praised God for His faithfulness (Lamentations 3:23). To be faithful is to do the right thing no matter what. Jeremiah was glad that even though God's people had not been faithful to Him, God stayed faithful to them. Even though He had to punish them, He had good plans for their future if they would just turn their hearts back to Him.

Enjoy Your Trip

Two Sides to the Story

Lamentations tells us two things that are equally true: God judges sin, *and* God is full of love. Just because one of those things is true doesn't mean the other isn't. God is holy, so He has to judge sin to stay true to Himself. But He loves us so much that He provides a way for our sin to be forgiven.

Where's the Gospel?

Because God made a promise to His people, He would bring them back home after seventy years of captivity in Babylon. God has made a promise to us too: After we live our lives here on earth, He'll take us home to heaven to be with Him and Jesus forever.

EZEKIEL

Check Your Location

Ezekiel wrote this book when he was taken captive to Babylon along with many other Israelites. In Babylon, Ezekiel preached to his people and told them to return to the Lord. God also gave Ezekiel a lot of strange visions that predicted the future!

Plot Your Course

Ezekiel's Calling (Ezekiel 1–3)

Ezekiel had trained to become a priest in the temple in Jerusalem, but then he was taken captive by the Babylonians. In Babylon, Ezekiel saw a wild vision of God in His glory. Then God called him to be His prophet. The Holy Spirit came inside Ezekiel and gave him the strength to tell the people what God told him.

CULTURE SHOCK

Ezekiel had a vision of God sitting on a sapphire throne (see Ezekiel 1). God appeared as a figure of fire and rainbow light. Below His throne were "four living creatures" (verse 5 NKJV) in a fiery cloud—a type of angel called *cherubim*. Each of them sort of looked human but had four faces (a man, an ox, an eagle, and a lion), four wings, and bronze calf hooves for feet. They moved like flashes of lightning, and each was followed by a wheel with a rim covered with eyes. Ezekiel hit the ground facedown in fear!

Ezekiel's Prophecies (Ezekiel 4—32)

The big thing Ezekiel told the people was why God let them be taken as prisoners to Babylon: so they would come back to Him to worship and obey Him. They had sinned against God, but He still wanted to have a relationship with them. It was also so they could understand that God is in control of everything. That means He can do whatever He wants!

Sometimes when God gave Ezekiel a message for the people, He told him to act out that message. Acting it out made the people remember it better. Here are some of the weird things Ezekiel did:

- shaved his head and beard
- laid on his side for more than a year
- baked bread using cow manure as fuel for the fire

God told Ezekiel about what was going to happen to other nations too—not just Israel. Many of these nations had even partied when Babylon defeated Israel, so now God was going to punish those nations.

Ezekiel's Good News (Ezekiel 33—48)

But this was the good news: God would restore Israel after their captivity.

First, they would come back home after seventy years in Babylon. Then, looking far into the future, Ezekiel saw what would happen to them in the end times (which still haven't happened yet). God will gather all the Jews together, and Israel will be at the center of Jesus's 1,000-year-long reign as King of the earth. They will have the coolest-looking temple ever!

Despite all the hard times Ezekiel predicted, God had a good plan for His people in the end. He has a good plan for you and me too, no matter how bad things may look.

Enjoy Your Trip

The Power of the Spirit

Ezekiel had a hard message to tell the people, but he was able to keep sharing that message because God's Holy Spirit entered him and gave him the power he needed. Because you are God's child, He gives you His Spirit to help you do hard things too.

Where's the Gospel?

In Ezekiel, God promised Israel that He would regenerate their hearts—make them new. This came true when Jesus lived on earth. Jesus told people that believing in Him is like being reborn (see John 3:3). He can make our hearts new, cleansing us of sin and giving us a new way of thinking and living.

▶ **God's Strange Commands to Ezekiel**

Read about these living illustrations in Ezekiel 3:1; 4:4-6; and 5:1.

DANIEL

Check Your Location

The prophet Daniel was born in Judah. But when he was a teenager, Babylon conquered Judah. Daniel was taken as a captive to Babylon. He lived in Babylon for the rest of his life—more than seventy years. Daniel served under several kings, starting with Nebuchadnezzar (try saying *that* five times fast!). Daniel's book has some of the most amazing stories and predictions you'll find in the whole Bible.

Plot Your Course

Not Your Normal History Lesson (Daniel 1–6)

The first half of Daniel's book tells us about his life.

When King Nebuchadnezzar attacked Judah, Daniel was still a teenager. He was taken captive to Babylon. From the beginning of his life there, Daniel followed God. When he was still young, he chose to follow all God's rules—*no matter where he was*. Daniel also interpreted a dream Nebuchadnezzar had with God's help and wisdom, so Nebuchadnezzar made Daniel a governor of his kingdom.

But Nebuchadnezzar wasn't always a nice guy. One time, he made a huge statue out of gold and told everyone to worship it. Three of Daniel's friends from back home—Shadrach, Meshach, and Abednego—refused, so the king threw them into a superheated furnace. But a fourth man appeared with them in the flames (probably Jesus), who kept them from burning up and delivered them.

Nebuchadnezzar praised God for saving Daniel's friends, but because he was a mighty king, he struggled with pride. God had to teach him a hard lesson. He caused Nebuchadnezzar to go insane and live outside like an animal for seven years. The king ate grass and grew really long hair and fingernails! God was showing that He is in control of our leaders here on earth, no matter who they are.

Nebuchadnezzar's grandson, Belshazzar, wasn't much better. Belshazzar threw a huge party. He disrespected God by using cups and pitchers he had stolen from God's temple in Jerusalem, so God caused a hand to appear and write a message on the wall. Daniel was very old by this point, but he came and interpreted the message: An empire called Medo-Persia was about to take over. It happened that very night. Say goodbye to Babylon!

The new king, Darius, made Daniel one of his governors to help him rule, but some men got jealous of Daniel. They had Darius pass a law saying that the people could only pray to Darius. Daniel prayed to God anyway, so he was thrown into a pit of lions as punishment! But guess what? God kept Daniel safe, showing He has the power to keep His people from harm.

Plenty of Powerful Prophecies (Daniel 7–12)

Predicting the future was a big part of Daniel's life and writings. The second half of his book tells us about the visions he had of the future. Some of these visions were given to him by angels, and some of these visions have already come true!

Here are some of the things Daniel predicted:

- The next biggest kingdoms in the world after Babylon would be Medo-Persia, Greece, and Rome.
- A man we call the Antichrist will rule in the end times, and Jesus will defeat him.

- A group of nations on earth will form a union in the end times, but God will break that union and set up His own eternal kingdom.

But one of the most amazing and important prophecies in the Bible is in Daniel 9. It predicts the exact day that the Messiah, Jesus Christ, would come to Jerusalem for the last time before He would be killed to save His people from sin. God's timing is perfect! That means we can trust Him all the time, just as Daniel did—even when life is scary.

CULTURE SHOCK

What do you think angels look like? Daniel saw an angel that had a body that glistened like a gem, flaming eyes, a face that flashed like lightning, and a voice like a huge chorus of people. Scary, huh? Daniel fainted when he saw him! That's why angels usually have to say, "Don't be afraid" when they appear to someone.

Enjoy Your Trip

Dare to Be a Daniel

Daniel wasn't afraid of what people thought of him or might do to him. Instead, he wanted to make God happy even while living in captivity! That meant he sometimes had to make hard choices and do the right thing no matter what. It was a daring and adventurous way to live! How can you dare to be like Daniel?

Where's the Gospel?

As we just saw, Daniel 9 is one of the most incredible prophecies about the Messiah. It predicted when Jesus would finish

God's greatest rescue mission—down to the day! All of history is about what Jesus did on the cross: He bought our salvation.

EXPECT THE UNEXPECTED

The prophecy in Daniel is so accurate that some skeptics say there's no way it could have been written down in Daniel's time. But if that were so, Daniel would have been no prophet, and his book would have been a forgery. But Jesus Himself called Daniel a prophet (Matthew 24:15), proving that Daniel's predictions are the real deal. That's because he got them from God.

▶ Daniel in the Lions' Den

Read about the world's greatest lion tamer in Daniel 6:13-23.

HOSEA, JOEL, AMOS, AND OBADIAH

Check Your Location

After Daniel, we begin a section of the Bible called the Minor Prophets. The previous guys (Isaiah, Jeremiah, Ezekiel, and Daniel) are known as the Major Prophets. "Major" doesn't mean better or more important than "Minor." It just means the books are longer.

The minor prophets all pack a powerful punch. They were the messengers God sent to warn Israel and Judah about the punishment for their sin. God wanted His people to turn from worshipping idols and come back to following Him alone. He said it in different ways through different prophets, but that's what He wanted to happen. God always wants to give us a chance to come back to Him.

Let's take a look at the first four minor prophets: Hosea, Joel, Amos, and Obadiah.

HOSEA

Plot Your Course

A Faithless Nation and a Faithful God (Hosea 1—14)

God didn't just call Hosea to be His prophet. God also told him to do something unusual and very difficult. He told Hosea to take a wife who was a prostitute.

So Hosea married a woman named Gomer. He gave her a

much better life, and they had kids together. But soon Gomer chased after other men. She was unfaithful to Hosea. That broke Hosea's heart.

But God told Hosea to go after Gomer, forgive her, and bring her back home. That's what God was going to do for Israel too. But first, Assyria was going to conquer them because of their disobedience. Israel had cheated on God spiritually. Now He was going to let them have what they wanted—idols.

The Assyrians worshipped idols, which are made-up gods that aren't even real. The Assyrians and their idols were not merciful or loving like God is. Israel would come to hate being under their control. They would want to come back to God. Hosea told them that God would forgive them and bring them back home one day. Even when we are unfaithful, God is always faithful.

Enjoy Your Trip

Where's the Gospel?

Hosea and Gomer's marriage is a picture of our relationship with God in the gospel story. Did you know that Hosea's name means "salvation"? Just like Gomer, we have left the One who loves us. We've sinned against Him. But God, like Hosea, has come after us. Through Jesus Christ, He forgives us of our sins, and we can belong to Him again!

JOEL

Plot Your Course

A Swarm of Judgment (Joel 1—3)

A swarm of locusts had attacked Israel. No one had ever experienced something so horrible. But something worse was coming.

God showed the prophet Joel how the army of Assyria would be like the locusts: They would destroy Israel. But after the Assyrians took Israel into captivity, God planned to restore His people. He would bring them back home (which He did).

But the destruction of the locusts also pointed to something else: the very end of the world. During the end times, the earth will experience something way worse than bugs or bullies. Joel called it "the day of the Lord." God will judge the earth.

God also told Joel that He has plans for Israel in the end times too. He will heal their land from plagues and damage. He will also heal their bodies and their broken hearts, and they will trust in Him. As hard as God's judgment is, His healing of His people will be wonderful. God will judge the earth.

CULTURE SHOCK

Imagine hearing a buzzing in the distance. You look up and see a cloud rising on the horizon. But the cloud is growing— and growing fast. The buzzing gets louder and louder. With a cold feeling in your gut, you realize it's not a rain cloud. It's a cloud of locusts, 100 feet high and four miles wide. They settle on every green thing. They chew and suck until nothing green is left. Your land looks like a fire has burned it down.

Enjoy Your Trip

Where's the Gospel?

Joel predicted that God was going to give us His Holy Spirit. And He did—after Jesus died, rose from the dead, and went back to heaven. As a believer, you have the Holy Spirit living in you. The Holy Spirit isn't a spooky type of ghost. He is God Himself, and He helps you live your life in a way that makes God happy.

AMOS

Plot Your Course

Tough Love (Amos 1—9)

Amos was a farmer from the southern kingdom of Judah. God told him to go to the northern kingdom of Israel and warn them about God's coming judgment for their sin.

Amos wasn't afraid to tell people his tough message. First, he described how God was angry with Israel's enemies—nations that had hurt His people. They were due for a dose of God's wrath. In other words, they were toast!

But then Amos said, "Judah and Israel are toast too!" God was fed up with His people's disobedience. So He was going to use other nations to punish them so that they would come back to Him.

But Amos saw God's faithful love as well. He saw that after God's wrath was over, God would bring Israel home. This shows us something very important about God: He can't just ignore sin. But He also wants to heal people who have been messed up by sin. Sometimes we need God's tough love.

Enjoy Your Trip

Where's the Gospel?

Amos's name means *burden-bearer*. Amos carried a heavy spiritual burden. His message was like a heavy weight on his heart. He had to tell his people that the punishment for their sin was on its way. Jesus Christ was a burden-bearer too. He carried the weight of our sins on the cross. And because of that, we no longer have to suffer the punishment for those sins!

OBADIAH

Plot Your Course

Payback for Pride (Obadiah 1—21)

Do you remember Jacob from the book of Genesis? Did you know he had a twin brother named Esau? Jacob and Esau didn't get along. Esau's descendants became a nation called Edom, and they didn't like Jacob's descendants, the Israelites.

But God told a man named Obadiah to speak against the Edomites. Edom had a strong capital city and a good defense system. But the Edomites were full of themselves because of it! So God told Obadiah to set them straight.

Why was God upset with Edom? Because Edom stood aside when the armies of Babylon attacked Jerusalem. Then they helped the Babylonians steal from and kill the Israelites.

But they wouldn't get away with it. Their pride and bullying would bring them down and lead to the destruction of their nation.

Obadiah also said that God was going to restore Israel one day. That won't happen until the end times, but when it does, it will be wonderful.

MUST-SEE SITES—*Petra*

The capital city of Edom was called Petra. It was carved into sandstone cliffs. You have to go down a narrow crack in a canyon to get there. For an army, that's hard to do. The Edomites felt safe in their rocky fortress, and they thought no one could ever defeat them. Petra still exists today, but no one has lived there for centuries. The Edomites are long gone, just as Obadiah predicted.

Enjoy Your Trip

Where's the Gospel?

Obadiah is a really short book, and it is focused on God's judgment on one neighboring nation, but Obadiah still points ahead to the Messiah, Jesus Christ. Obadiah 21 says that "the Lord himself will be king" one day. This will happen when Jesus comes back a second time to make the world right again.

JONAH

Check Your Location

Jonah lived in the northern kingdom of Israel, not far from Nazareth (where Jesus later grew up). At the time, Israel wasn't obeying the Lord. God was soon going to let their enemy Assyria come and conquer them. But first, God told Jonah to tell those same Assyrians to repent of *their* sin! You probably know the story: Jonah didn't like that one bit, so he tried running away from God. Bad move! Jonah would have to face a fishy foe before learning that God's plans can't be stopped.

Plot Your Course

Running from God (Jonah 1)

God told Jonah to go preach to Nineveh, the capital city of Assyria. But Jonah got on a boat and went the opposite way. He didn't want to obey God!

You'd think as God's prophet, Jonah would know better. You can't escape God. He's everywhere and knows everything. God sent a bad storm to get Jonah's attention while he was on the ship. But instead of asking God to forgive him for his disobedience, Jonah told the sailors to throw him overboard. They didn't want to, but finally they did. The sea calmed down right away.

Then God sent a fish to swallow Jonah. God had a job for Jonah to do, so He kept him safe in the belly of this fish.

MUST-SEE SITES—*Nineveh*

Nineveh was the mighty capital city of the Assyrian Empire. It was surrounded by massive walls. It took three days to walk across the city. Like most cities, it was a mix of the best and worst of humankind's accomplishments. Nineveh was well-known for being violent and scary. Assyrian kings dragged their captives by pierced lips for hundreds of miles. They peeled the skin off other captives and piled their heads up outside the city gates.[2]

Running to God (Jonah 2—3)

After three whole days and nights in the fish, Jonah finally cried out to the Lord. He prayed a prayer that was full of Bible verses. Jonah knew the Bible really well from memory—but that didn't mean he obeyed it!

Jonah admitted to God that he had messed up and was getting what he deserved, so God made the fish vomit him up on the beach. Nasty! Even after all this, God gave Jonah a second chance. Because God loves to pardon people, He told Jonah again to go preach to the people in Nineveh.

This time, Jonah obeyed. He went to the city and told the people God's message: "Nineveh is going to be destroyed in forty days!"

And something absolutely amazing happened. One hundred percent of the Ninevites believed God and turned away from their sin and evil ways! So God held back His judgment and didn't destroy Nineveh.

CULTURE SHOCK

God might have used the superstitions of the Ninevites to get their attention. They worshipped a fake god named Dagon,

---

[2] Daniel David Luckenbill, *Ancient Records of Assyria and Babylonia*, 2 vols. (Chicago: University of Chicago Press, 1926–1927), sections 599, 800, and 810.

who supposedly controlled the seas. Imagine Jonah showing up in Nineveh. He had just been belched from the belly of a great fish. Maybe he was even bleached white by the digestive juices in its stomach. That would get their attention!

Run-In with God (Jonah 4)

Nineveh's change of heart was worth celebrating! But guess what? Jonah got angry! He knew that God loves to forgive people of their sins. That's why Jonah didn't want to go to Nineveh in the first place. He wanted his enemies to be punished.

But God was—and is—full of mercy. God didn't give the Ninevites the punishment they deserved for their sin. Instead, God showed them kindness. After all, He made them and loved them. God doesn't want anyone to die without coming to know and believe in Him.

Enjoy Your Trip

Dealing with Ninevites

Is there anyone who makes you really angry or who you even sometimes wish would get hurt? When you feel like this, remember that God loves to forgive people's sins and be kind to them even when they don't deserve it. How can you be like God and show kindness to somebody?

Where's the Gospel?

The book of Jonah shows how far God will go to let a city full of people know He wants to forgive them. Hundreds of years after the story of Jonah, Jesus Christ proved just how far. He went to the farthest lengths ever to offer forgiveness to the entire world: He died on the cross!

MICAH, NAHUM, AND HABAKKUK

Check Your Location

The next three minor prophets shared a message similar to the first group's: God was bringing judgment on His people (and their enemies). But He would also bring them back to their land eventually. And in the future, He would give Israel a special place in the world government, which will be ruled by Jesus Christ. Let's see what Micah, Nahum, and Habakkuk had to say.

MICAH

Plot Your Course

Fishing for Worms (Micah 1–7)

The prophet Micah pointed out the sins of Samaria and Jerusalem, the capital cities of Israel and Judah. Their leaders were like worms at the center of an apple. They made the whole nation rotten from the core! They guided the people in doing bad things, like worshipping idols, stealing from the poor, and hurting others.

But God wasn't going to let them get away with it. Micah warned that God was going to expose them and use Israel's enemies to judge them.

Micah spoke a lot about how Israel would be restored after this judgment. God had made promises to be faithful to Israel no matter what. After the Israelites lived in captivity for a while, they would return home. Then during the end times—the end of the world—the Messiah will come back to earth and make everything right.

Micah made some predictions about this Messiah, who we know is Jesus Christ. Micah said Jesus would be born in the little town of Bethlehem, and guess what? Hundreds of years later, He was!

Enjoy Your Trip

Do the Right Thing

God reminded His people of what makes Him happy: "[God] has told you what he wants, and this is all it is: to be fair, just, merciful, and to walk humbly with your God" (Micah 6:8 TLB). God *doesn't* just want you to sit around and learn a lot about Him. He wants you to *do* what you know to be good and true. Otherwise, you're doing no good at all!

Where's the Gospel?

Micah predicted that the Messiah would be like a shepherd, feeding and protecting His people (look up Micah 5:2-4). Jesus Himself said, "I am the good shepherd. The good shepherd sacrifices his life for the sheep" (John 10:11). And He did just that on the cross, giving His life for us so that our sins can be forgiven.

NAHUM

Plot Your Course

What Goes Around Comes Around (Nahum 1–3)

Nahum spoke against Israel's enemy, Assyria. He predicted that their capital city, Nineveh, was going to be wrecked. This was 150 years after Jonah had brought an amazing revival to the city. The Ninevites had gone back to their old ways and were even worse than they were before. So God was going to make an end of them.

Nahum warned the mighty Ninevite army that doom was coming. God would shatter their mighty empire. Nahum even predicted that a flood would come to Nineveh (see Nahum 1:8). Not long afterward, the Tigris River rose to destroy some of the city walls. That let other armies attack Nineveh. Pretty amazing!

Nahum described some of the city's awful behavior. His examples proved that God had good reason to judge the people and put an end to their evil.

And there was nothing they could do about it. They had the opportunity to turn and follow God. But because they decided to reject Him, their fate was sealed.

EXPECT THE UNEXPECTED

Here's something interesting Nahum told us about God: He is "jealous" (Nahum 1:2). But His jealousy isn't like human jealousy. Think of it like this: God is the only true God, right? He is the one who made the earth. He is all-powerful and all-knowing. God is jealous because He doesn't like it when His people aren't completely following Him. He wants you to follow Him with your whole heart. He deserves it!

Enjoy Your Trip

Where's the Gospel?

God showed grace to Nineveh in Jonah's day. But then the people went back to their evil ways, so He brought judgment on them. It's the same thing with the gospel. God showed us grace by sending Jesus to die on the cross for us. But if we reject Jesus and go back to sinning, we will have to face God's judgment for our sin.

That doesn't mean you can't make mistakes. But if you are really following Jesus, you will ask Him to forgive you when you make a mistake. Then you will try not to make the same mistake again.

HABAKKUK

Plot Your Course

Hardship and Hope (Habakkuk 1—3)

Habakkuk was both a prophet and a priest. Habakkuk wrote his book like he was having a conversation with God. The people of Judah kept turning away from God. Habakkuk couldn't believe that God hadn't done anything about it. So Habakkuk prayed and waited to hear from God.

God finally replied: He was going to let Babylon attack Judah. This was not what Habakkuk expected or hoped to hear!

But God told Habakkuk something else: Even though Babylon would come and punish Judah, God would one day punish Babylon! And not only that, but one day at the very end of time, God will make everything right for all His people.

Habakkuk was terrified of what was going to happen to him and his people. But even though God was going to let them suffer for a little while, Habakkuk praised Him and found joy in Him. He knew that God works even the very worst things together into something good. He wrote a song that celebrated God's good plans for His people in the end—like the plans He has for you and me too!

PACK SMART

Even when you do your best to follow God, bad things can still happen to you. When that happens, some Christians get mad at God. We don't know why God let it happen. But that's why it's so important to hold on to what you *do* know. You know that God is good. You know that He has a plan for your life. You know that He loves you. The Bible says these things over and over. You know they are true. So when bad things happen, the real question isn't "Why, God?" but "Will You help me trust You, God?"

Enjoy Your Trip

Where's the Gospel?

Habakkuk 2:4 says, "The righteous will live by their faithfulness to God." This is a very important verse in the Bible. It tells us how the gospel works. We are not saved because we do good things or have a lot of money or friends. We are saved only because we have faith in Jesus Christ. We trust that He took the punishment for our sins on the cross.

ZEPHANIAH AND HAGGAI

Check Your Location

The next two minor prophets carried the same message as the rest. Zephaniah was a last-minute prophet. He preached to the people of Judah right before the kingdom fell to the superpower of the world—Babylon. He warned them that because they weren't following God anymore, the Babylonians were on their way.

Haggai was the first prophet God sent to speak to the Jews after their exile into Babylon. They left after seventy years and returned to Jerusalem. Haggai encouraged them to put God first by rebuilding the temple so they could worship God. Babylon's armies had destroyed the first temple and burned part of the city. It was going to take lots of hard work and determination to rebuild it.

ZEPHANIAH

Plot Your Course

The Last Wake-Up Call (Zephaniah 1–3)

Zephaniah tried to wake up Judah to their sin—the things they had done that would bring God's judgment. A lot of people were worshipping God, but they were also worshipping other gods from other nations. God wants His people to worship Him alone. Only He deserves to be worshipped.

So God was going to correct Judah's behavior by letting Babylon come and invade. Zephaniah described God in an interesting way—as one who wounds His people in order to heal them. Sounds weird, doesn't it?

Think of God like a surgeon who has to make a cut on someone's body. Ouch! But the surgeon does it to cure that person of a deadly disease. God was acting like a surgeon. The cut was the Babylonian invasion, but God was doing it to keep His people from the deadly disease of sinning against Him.

Sadly, Zephaniah's wake-up call didn't work. In the end, after the Babylonian invasion and captivity, God would forgive His people and bring them home. So Zephaniah ended his book with lots of joy.

Enjoy Your Trip

Where's the Gospel?

God is not only just (or fair)—He's also full of mercy and forgiveness. This is what Zephaniah shows us. God was going to bring justice by punishing His people's sin, but then He would make things right again. In the same way, Jesus took on the horrible judgment for our sin. But then He made things right again. Now we can know God and be with Him in heaven forever!

HAGGAI

Plot Your Course

A Prophet's Pep Talk (Haggai 1—2)

After their exile in Babylon, the Jews were set free to go rebuild the temple and walls of Jerusalem. The temple was the special place where the people gathered to worship God and make animal sacrifices to Him.

They began the project with lots of excitement. But everywhere they looked, they saw broken walls and burned houses. After a while, they got discouraged and stopped building.

God sent the prophets Haggai and Zechariah to inspire the people. Haggai pointed out the reasons they were struggling:

First, they were being selfish. They wanted to build their own homes, not God's temple. They needed to put God first, and He would provide for them.

Second, they were sad that the temple wasn't going to be as amazing as the old one King Solomon built. But God's presence would still be there, and that's what counted most.

Third, they needed to confess their secret sins. God wanted them to have clean hearts to worship Him.

Finally, they were guilty of unbelief. There were local people who didn't want them to build the temple. The Jews didn't believe God would protect them from these enemies.

But God encouraged Zerubbabel, the leader of the people. He told him, "I have chosen you" (Haggai 2:23). God would help Zerubbabel get the job done. That's how God works. He promises to bless those who obey Him and do His work. Zerubbabel then went and encouraged the people to keep working.

Enjoy Your Trip

Where's the Gospel?

Zerubbabel was a special person. He had God's special stamp of approval to be the builder of the temple. This was because Zerubbabel was descended from King David. That meant he was also an ancestor of Jesus Christ! God told Zerubbabel, "I will shake all nations, and they shall come to the Desire of All Nations" (Haggai 2:7 NKJV).

That was a prophecy. God called Jesus "the Desire of All Nations." He was saying that Jesus, Zerubbabel's descendant, would come back and rule the world in the end times. Jesus will shake things up, overthrowing all the nations of the world who want to rule. He will rule the world Himself as our true King.

ZECHARIAH AND MALACHI

Check Your Location

The last two minor prophets are Zechariah and Malachi. Zechariah was born in Babylon during Israel's captivity. He moved to Jerusalem with his family after the Jews' captivity was over. Along with Haggai, Zechariah preached to the Jews to inspire them to rebuild their temple. He also made predictions about a lot of things that would happen in the future. He talked especially about the Messiah, Jesus Christ.

Malachi lived during the time of Nehemiah, who helped rebuild the temple when the Jews returned home from Babylon. His book is the last book in the Old Testament. And he was the last prophet God spoke to for a long time. It would be 400 years until the next prophet showed up.

ZECHARIAH

Plot Your Course

Facing Challenges with God's Help (Zechariah 1–14)

God used Zechariah for two purposes. First, He wanted to comfort Israel after their captivity in Babylon. Second, He wanted to encourage the people to finish building the temple.

God gave Zechariah a bunch of visions about rebuilding the temple. These visions were sometimes pretty bizarre! They used symbols to show the challenges Israel was facing. But they also showed how God would help His people through the tough times by the power of His Spirit.

Then God gave Zechariah lots of predictions about Jesus's first and second comings. He made these predictions more than 500 years before Jesus came the first time. The first time Jesus came, He gave His life to save us from sin. Then He went back to heaven. But Jesus is going to come a second time. When He does, He'll put a stop to evil, punish Israel's enemies, and bring peace to the whole world. What a great message!

CULTURE SHOCK

Zechariah had some really weird visions. One of the weirdest was of a woman in a basket (see Zechariah 5:5-11). Her name was Wickedness, and she was a symbol of sin. Two winged women carried her off in the basket to Babylon. What did this crazy vision mean?

By carrying Wickedness away, the winged women were showing the Jews a new way to live. They needed to abandon all the evil habits and ways of worship that they had seen and learned back in Babylon. God wanted to do a new work in their hearts and lives now that they had returned to Israel.

Enjoy Your Trip

Where's the Gospel?

No other minor prophet book predicts more about Jesus than Zechariah. Zechariah had visions of Jesus's first and second coming. Sometimes the visions came one right after another! Zechariah 9:9 says the Messiah would ride into

Jerusalem on the colt of a donkey. Jesus did that at the beginning of His last week on earth (see Luke 19:29-37). Then in the very next verse, Zechariah 9:10 says that the Messiah will end all wars and bring peace. Jesus will do that when He comes back to earth a second time.

MALACHI

Plot Your Course

True Love Means Telling the Truth (Malachi 1—4)

This book is a conversation between God and the people of Israel. God spoke through the prophet Malachi. He began by telling Israel, "I have always loved you" (Malachi 1:2). The people didn't really believe in His love, but God still made it clear—He truly did love them.

Then God laid out Israel's sins in front of them. He didn't like their cheating, their laziness, their bad marriages, their divorce, their stealing, their pride, and how they didn't give any of their money back to the Lord. Plus, they had excuses for every sinful thing they did! But God *still* loved them. He was still going to send them a deliverer who would forgive all their sins, the Messiah Jesus Christ.

In fact, Malachi shows us an awesome link to Jesus. The last word in his book—and the whole Old Testament—is "curse" (Malachi 4:6). This curse is the result of sin. Sin infects every single person who has ever been born. Sin is why Jesus had to come to earth. He was the only one who could take away the curse of sin. Here at the very end of the Old Testament, the stage is now set for the Bible's main character, Jesus, to come into the world. The cure for the curse was on the way!

Enjoy Your Trip

Where's the Gospel?

Malachi predicted that a messenger would come along and clear the way for the Messiah. This messenger was John the Baptist, who told the people that the Messiah was coming. You don't have to wait 400 years to see who He is. You can just turn the page and meet the long-awaited Messiah, Jesus Christ! He is God's message to humankind, a message of love, forgiveness, and hope.

MATTHEW AND MARK

Check Your Location

After the last book of the Old Testament, Malachi, a lot happened in the world. But God kept silent for 400 years. The Gospels broke that silence. The Gospels are the first four books in the New Testament: Matthew, Mark, Luke, and John. In this chapter, we'll look at Matthew and Mark.

Matthew gives us our first look at Jesus Christ. Jesus is the person who is at the center of not just the Bible but all of history. Matthew shows us that Jesus is the Messiah (the Chosen One) and King of the Jews. Eventually, Jesus will be King of the whole world.

We think John Mark wrote the Gospel of Mark. He was a relative of Barnabas in the book of Acts and traveled on mission trips with Paul and Peter. Most scholars agree that Mark got a lot of his information from Peter.[3] His Gospel is the shortest and might be the earliest one written.

MATTHEW

Plot Your Course

The King Has Come (Matthew 1)

When Matthew told the story of Jesus's birth, he made sure to connect it to prophecy. Hundreds of years before Jesus was

---

[3] Peter Williams, "The Historical Reliability of Mark's Gospel," 2008, Theology Network, http://www.theologynetwork.org/biblical-studies/the-historical-reliability-of-marks-gospel.htm.

born, the prophet Isaiah predicted that God would come as a baby, grow up, and then save His people (look up Matthew 1:23). An angel told Joseph, Jesus's earthly father, to name Mary's special baby *Jesus*. The name Jesus means "God Saves." The Jewish people had been waiting a long time for their Messiah to come!

> **LEARN THE LANGUAGE—*Christ***
>
> When Jesus came to earth, He was simply known as Jesus of Nazareth. *Christ* is His title, not His last name. *Christ* is a Greek word that means the same thing as the Jewish word *Messiah*: "The Anointed One." Being anointed means being chosen by God for His work. Jesus was chosen to do God's greatest work: salvation!

The King Is Presented (Matthew 2–3)

Some people were excited about Jesus coming, and some weren't. A group of astrologers from the Middle East were thrilled. They followed an unusual star all the way to Bethlehem to come find the baby who was the new king of the Jews. But the Romans were in charge of Israel in those days. And the local king of Israel at the time, Herod, was not happy about this news.

Herod didn't want anyone else to be king, so he killed all the boys two years old and younger in and around Bethlehem (where the prophet Micah predicted that the Messiah would be born). An angel warned Joseph to take Jesus and Mary to live in Egypt until Herod died. They moved back to Israel when Jesus was older.

When Jesus grew up, He began His ministry. His cousin, John the Baptist, had been telling people to turn from their sins and be baptized because "the Kingdom of Heaven is near" (Matthew 3:2).

One day, John saw Jesus, and God showed him the truth: Jesus wasn't just his cousin but also his Lord, the Messiah! Jesus told John to baptize Him, and John obeyed even though he knew he was the one who needed to be baptized by Jesus.

The King and His Kingdom (Matthew 4—25)

Jesus began to teach the people about the kingdom of God. He gave a famous teaching called the Sermon on the Mount. He talked about the kind of behavior that pleases God and challenged people to make sure their hearts were in the right place with God. He also told special stories (called parables) about how to live in God's kingdom.

Jesus also healed people who were sick, disabled, or possessed by demons. Jesus's teaching and miracles made a lot of people happy, but some of the Jewish leaders were upset.

CULTURE SHOCK

Jesus didn't say you had to *like* your enemies. But He did say to *love* them (Matthew 5:43-48). So how do you love an enemy? Ask God to bless them, no matter how they've treated you. Say, "God, please change this person's heart. Help them to get to know You." It's not easy. But because you're obeying God, He will help you do it. More important, He will keep your heart from becoming bitter and mean.

The King Finishes the Task (Matthew 26—28)

The Jewish religious leaders didn't like that Jesus was becoming so popular. They often tried to trick Him into saying the wrong thing. But Jesus was a lot smarter than they were and didn't fall for their traps. They accused Jesus of claiming to be God. He agreed that He was God, but they didn't believe

Him. They arrested Jesus, had Him beaten, and then talked the Romans into killing Him.

The Romans nailed Jesus to a cross. When He died, His friends buried Him in a stone cave, called a tomb. They were scared and sad—but God had other plans! He brought Jesus back to life. That proved once and for all that Jesus was the Messiah, the one God had chosen to save people from their sins. Because Jesus rose from the dead, anyone who puts their faith in Him can be saved. Jesus accomplished God's rescue mission, finishing the task of our salvation!

After Jesus rose from the dead, He appeared to His friends and gave them a special mission of their own: "Go and make disciples of all the nations" (Matthew 28:19). He promised He would always be with His followers, even if they couldn't see Him. Then He sent them out to change the world.

TOUR GUIDE

- I delivered one of the most important messages people have ever heard.
- I was called the greatest of all men ever born.
- I ate a pretty crazy diet and wore uncomfortable clothes.
- Read Matthew 3:1-4 and Matthew 11:10-11 to find out who I am.

Enjoy Your Trip

What Does It Mean to Be Blessed?

The world's idea of what it means to be blessed—having health, wealth, and beauty—is the opposite of what Jesus taught in the Sermon on the Mount. He said that being blessed—being truly happy—comes from realizing how much we need God (see Matthew 5:2-12). God honors those who humble themselves and seek Him.

The Golden Rule

Jesus said how we treat others is super important to God (see Matthew 7:12). The Golden Rule sets Christianity apart from all other religions. Instead of *not* doing what you *don't* want others to do to you, Jesus told us to *do* the right thing—to be loving, kind, and gracious. Is that how you treat others?

Where's the Gospel?

The key word in Matthew's Gospel is *fulfilled*. Jesus fulfilled prophecy after prophecy about the Messiah, so Matthew wrote down these Old Testament prophecies. He wanted to convince his Jewish audience that Jesus is the one they had been waiting for to save them.

▶ Do Not Judge

Read about Jesus's object lesson in Matthew 7:1-5.

MARK

Plot Your Course

God's Servant Goes to Work (Mark 1—9)

Mark focuses on Jesus as a busy worker and servant of the Lord. His Gospel is like an action movie of Jesus's life. It moves quickly from scene to scene, telling us what Jesus said and did. Mark included a lot less of Jesus's teaching and more of Jesus in action. Jesus was on a rescue mission to save humankind from sin. Mark shows Him doing His job.

Mark tells us that after John baptized Jesus, Jesus went out into the desert and overcame being tempted by Satan. Then Jesus began telling people about God's good news of salvation. He called His first disciples to follow Him. He cast out an evil spirit, healed Peter's mother-in-law and a lot of other people, and preached in Galilee. Then He healed another man of a horrible disease called leprosy. And that was just *chapter 1*!

In the next several chapters, Jesus stayed busy. He used miracles to heal people and feed thousands. He sent demons out of people and blessed little children. But His enemies didn't like what He was doing. They didn't like that He claimed to be God, so they made plans to kill Him.

EXPECT THE UNEXPECTED

One time, the disciples got into an argument over which of them was the best—after Jesus, of course (look up Mark 9:33-37). Jesus told them that God's kingdom doesn't work like that. He said, "Whoever wants to be first must take last place and be the servant of everyone else" (Mark 9:35). To be great in Jesus's eyes is to put other people first.

God's Servant Finishes His Work (Mark 10–16)

Mark spent almost half of his Gospel writing about the final week of Jesus's life on earth. During this time, Jesus was betrayed, arrested, tortured, crucified, and resurrected. That's quite a week!

The last week of Jesus's life is the most important part of the Bible. That's because everything in the Old Testament led up to Jesus's death on the cross. After Adam and Eve messed up in the Garden of Eden, God cursed Satan. He told Satan that He would send someone special to defeat him and undo all the evil Satan had done. That "someone special" was Jesus. And Jesus defeated Satan at the cross!

That's why the word *gospel* means "good news." It's good news that God loved us enough to send His Son to die in our place so we can be free from sin. But that freedom was very expensive. It cost Jesus His life.

Even though the Romans used crucifixion to kill criminals, Jesus was not a criminal. He is the only person to never do anything wrong in His life! But if Jesus was innocent, why did He end up on a cross? Because God wanted Him there.

The cross was God's plan all along. When Jesus was betrayed by His friend Judas and handed over to His enemies, God didn't say, "Oh no, I never thought that would happen! What do I do now?" God sent Jesus to earth *knowing* that He would have to suffer to finish His mission. And Jesus knew it too. He did it because He loves God and He loves you. The cross was how He showed that love.

Mark's story ends with Jesus's resurrection. Before Jesus went back to heaven, He gave His followers a mission of their own: "Go into all the world and preach the Good News to everyone" (Mark 16:15).

Enjoy Your Trip

Where's the Gospel?

The key word in Mark's Gospel is *immediately*. Jesus was God's obedient servant. He didn't sit around and make excuses. He served God by serving others (look up Mark 10:45). When you believe in Jesus as Lord and Savior, He immediately saves you. Then you go out and serve God by serving others, just like Jesus did.

LUKE AND JOHN

Check Your Location

Luke and John are the third and fourth Gospels. Luke's Gospel was written by a Greek medical doctor named Luke. His book tells the longest and most complete story of Jesus Christ's life. Luke wanted his readers to see that Jesus was not just fully God but fully human. Jesus is the only perfect man who ever lived.

Most people believe that the apostle John wrote the Gospel of John. John was Jesus's closest friend. He called himself "the disciple Jesus loved" (John 13:23). John was there for all three years of Jesus's ministry on earth. He watched Jesus die on the cross, and he saw Jesus after He came back to life. The most-used words in his book are *Jesus Christ* and *believe*. John really wanted us to believe that Jesus is the Christ, the Son of the living God.

LUKE

Plot Your Course

Meet the Messiah (Luke 1–4)

Luke started with the wonderful birth of Jesus. An angel appeared to a young woman named Mary and told her that she would have a child who would save His people. So Mary sang a beautiful song of praise to God. Then she and her fiancé, Joseph, traveled to Bethlehem, where Jesus, the Messiah, was born. Luke said that angels filled the sky and praised God, and some shepherds came to visit.

Jesus had an amazing birth, but it was just the beginning of the most amazing life that has ever been lived!

PACK SMART

The only verse in the Bible that talks about Jesus growing up is Luke 2:52: "Jesus grew both tall and wise, and was loved by God and man" (TLB). Even as a kid, Jesus loved God, His Father. He studied the Bible and lived according to what He learned. That helped things go well for Him as He grew up.

The Messiah's Methods (Luke 4—21)

When Luke was writing his Gospel, God inspired him to talk to people who had seen Jesus in action. Luke interviewed them, wrote down their stories, and then put them in order. He wanted to make sure he had the facts straight. As a result, he recorded some wonderful stories that aren't found in any of the other Gospels. Here are a few of them:

- Jesus told the parable (or story) of a son who wasted all his money and did foolish things, but his dad welcomed him home anyway, just like God our Father does for us (look up Luke 15:11-32).
- Jesus also told a parable of how even though Samaritans and Jews were enemies, a Samaritan helped a hurt Jewish traveler when two Jewish men wouldn't (look up Luke 10:25-37).
- After Jesus's resurrection, He walked in disguise along a road with two of His followers. He told them

how the birth, death, and resurrection of the Messiah had been predicted by the Old Testament (look up Luke 24:13-32). This is one of my favorite stories about Jesus!

The Messiah's Mission (Luke 22—24)

As a doctor, Luke talked a lot about Jesus's healing ministry too. As a perfect man, Jesus truly cared for people and did all He could to help them. He taught them God's ways and healed them from sickness and injury.

When the time came, Jesus helped all people in the most important way possible. He let Himself be arrested, beaten, and nailed to a cross. He died so our sins could be forgiven.

Jesus knew that all of His suffering would be worth it. He knew God would raise Him from the dead, showing that death can be defeated and sin can be forgiven when we trust in Jesus. All the pain and trouble were worth it to Him because every single human being is worth it to Him. *You* are worth it to Him!

MUST-SEE SITES—*Golgotha*

The hill where Jesus was crucified was called Golgotha in Greek. The name means "Skull Hill" because it looks like a skull. The name in Latin is *Calvariae Locus*, where we get the English word *Calvary*. It seems like a good name for a place where people were often killed.

TOUR GUIDE

- In keeping with Jewish custom, I was engaged to be married when I was between twelve and fourteen years old.

- I wrote a worship song about how great God is to keep His promises.
- Being a mom turned out to be much harder than I thought it would be.
- Read Luke 1:26-38, Luke 1:46-55, and Luke 2:33-35 to find out who I am.

Enjoy Your Trip

Where's the Gospel?

The key phrase in Luke's Gospel is *Son of Man*. Luke showed that Jesus was not just a *good* man but the *God*-man. Jesus was fully God and fully human, so Luke called Him the "Son of Man." That means that Jesus knows exactly how we feel. He knows what makes us happy, sad, nervous, scared, or angry. But because He is also God, He can help us. He makes us enjoy our good times even more, and He helps us get through our hard times with hope.

▶ True Greatness

Read about Jesus's attitude toward little children in Luke 9:46-48.

JOHN

Plot Your Course

The Son of God Was God the Son (John 1—4)

John began his Gospel in a mysterious way. He wrote, "In the beginning the Word already existed. The Word was with God, and the Word was God" (John 1:1). That sounds cool, but it's also pretty strange! What was this "Word"?

John told us, "The Word became human and made his home among us" (verse 14). That's *Jesus*! Jesus is the Word of God, and He is also the Son of God. Jesus came to the world He made and lived here for a while. Why? To save the people He created. Wow!

When Jesus began His ministry as an adult, He showed up at the Jordan River. John the Baptist saw Him and called Him the Lamb of God who would take away the world's sins (see John 1:29).

Then Jesus got to work. He called His disciples, did miracles, and taught people about the Bible. Jesus did things that other people didn't dare to do. He made people wonder, "Who is this guy?"

A man named Nicodemus tried to find out. He came one night to talk to Jesus. Jesus got right to the most important point: how to get to heaven. He told Nicodemus, "Unless you are born again, you can never get into the Kingdom of God" (John 3:3 TLB).

Jesus then told Nicodemus how we can be born again: "God loved the world so much that he gave his only Son so that anyone who believes in him shall not perish but have eternal life" (John 3:16 TLB).

This famous verse, John 3:16, tells us why and how God

saved us. God saved us because He loves us. He loves us so much that He sent the person who means the most to Him—His only Son, Jesus—to die for us. All we have to do is believe in Jesus to be saved. And when we decide to put our faith in Jesus, God gives us a new start. It's like we're being born again!

The Son of God Makes Enemies (John 5–12)

As Jesus made Himself known, His enemies began to plot how to get rid of Him. Most of the Jewish people didn't believe that Jesus was the Messiah, and all the miracles Jesus did made Him a target for the religious leaders. The conflict between them and Jesus grew and grew—until they wanted to kill Him!

The Son of God Teaches Children of God (John 13–17)

Shortly before the final week of His life, Jesus stopped doing His work in public. Instead, He focused on His twelve closest followers. Jesus knew His time was short, so He wanted to share some important words with His friends at their last Passover together.

After they ate dinner, Jesus filled a large bowl with water and washed each of His disciples' feet. He wanted to show His friends how they should love and serve one another. Then Jesus encouraged them to trust in Him and in God. He told them that hard times would come in their lives, but they shouldn't worry, because He had defeated the world. The victory He would win at the cross would give them the power to overcome hard times.

PACK SMART

The Holy Spirit is the friend that Jesus sent to be with you as you follow Him (look up John 16:5-15). The Holy Spirit is God, just like God the Father and Jesus the Son. When you say yes to Jesus as your Lord and Savior, the Holy Spirit comes to live in your heart and help you. He is also called the Advocate (the one who sticks up for you), the Counselor (the one who gives you good advice), and the Encourager (the one who helps you face hard times with hope).

The Son of God Suffers to Save (John 18—19)

Jesus knew what was coming—His suffering and death—and He knew it would be hard. But this was the moment He was born for. Then His disciple Judas betrayed Him. Judas told Jesus's enemies where to find Him, and He was arrested in the Garden of Gethsemane. Jesus could have called angels to come rescue Him, but He didn't. He let Himself be arrested.

Then Jesus was taken to the high priest of the Jews. The priest couldn't find an excuse to kill Jesus, so he sent Jesus to the Roman governor, Pontius Pilate. Pilate questioned Jesus but couldn't find anything wrong with Him. Even so, Pilate gave the Jews what they wanted: He had Jesus crucified.

Jesus was nailed to the cross and went through horrible pain and suffering. After several hours, He said, "It is finished!" and died (John 19:30). Nicodemus and his friend, Joseph of Arimathea, buried Jesus's body in a tomb Joseph owned.

The Son of God Conquers Death (John 20—21)

Three days later, Jesus's friend Mary Magdalene went to the tomb. She found the huge stone that had covered the entrance pushed aside—and the tomb was empty! She ran and told the disciples, who came and saw for themselves. They believed that Jesus was risen, but they didn't understand that the Bible said Jesus must die and rise again to save us.

A little later, Jesus appeared to His friends, including John. Jesus was alive! He looked the same and had a body they could touch. He had healed from His beating. But He still had the holes in His hands and side from when He was crucified. But now they were marks of His victory over death.

John then explained why he wrote his Gospel (read John 20:31). He wanted you to know that you can have eternal life if you believe Jesus died for your sins and rose again.

Enjoy Your Trip

Where's the Gospel?

The key phrase in John's Gospel is *Son of God*. The most amazing thing about Jesus is that He is God in human form. Seven times in John's Gospel, Jesus said something about Himself that began with the words "I am." If you remember, "I AM" is the name God gave Himself when He met Moses (look up Exodus 3:14). When Jesus said, "I am," He was really saying, "I AM God."

And that was John's focus in this book. He used the title *Jesus Christ* (*Christ* meaning "the Anointed One" or "Messiah") about 170 times. He also used the word *believe* about 100 times. John's main idea rings loud and clear: Jesus is God, and here's why you should believe in Him.

ACTS

Check Your Location

The book of Acts was written by Luke as a sequel to his Gospel. Acts tells the story of the first thirty years after Jesus returned to heaven. During this time, the Christian church got started, and the earliest mission trips began. The Holy Spirit gave the believers in the early church strength and power as they followed the orders Jesus gave them: "You will be my witnesses, telling people about me everywhere" (Acts 1:8).

Plot Your Course

Sharing the Gospel in Jerusalem (Acts 1—7)

After Jesus's resurrection, He told His followers what to do next and then went back up to heaven.

First, the believers had to wait for the Holy Spirit, since Jesus had promised that He would send Him. The Holy Spirit made an impressive entrance. The believers were all in a room together. There was a loud sound like a roaring wind. Then something that looked like a little flame appeared above each person's head. The Holy Spirit had come!

Filled with courage and led by the apostle Peter, the believers went out into the streets of Jerusalem. They began to tell everyone they met about who Jesus was and all He had done to save them. Many people began to follow the Lord that day.

The Gospel Gets a New Champion (Acts 8—13)

Soon the gospel spread outside of Jerusalem. God chose an unusual man to help spread the good news around the world: Saul of Tarsus. The problem was that Saul hated Christians! His job was to hunt them down and arrest them. But God had other plans for Saul.

One day, Saul was riding his horse to Damascus when a bright light appeared. He fell off his horse, blinded. He heard a voice say, "Saul! Saul! Why are you persecuting me?" (Acts 9:4). It was Jesus!

After this incredible encounter with Jesus, Saul became a believer in Him. He started going by the name *Paul*. Soon Paul was going all over the place, sharing the good news of Christ. Paul's story tells us that God can save and use *anyone*!

Getting the Word Out into the World (Acts 14—28)

In Jerusalem, evil King Herod began persecuting the church. Among other things, he had Peter arrested. But an angel broke Peter out of prison, and Peter continued to lead the church and tell people about Jesus.

Meanwhile, Paul prepared to share the gospel in as many places as he could. He made three separate trips to spread the good news of Jesus. These are called Paul's missionary journeys. A missionary is someone God sends on a mission to talk about Jesus with anyone who will listen. The rest of Acts focuses mostly on Paul's work as a missionary.

Paul's First Missionary Journey (Acts 13—14)

On the first missionary journey, Paul and a believer named Barnabas went to Antioch. But they were chased out of town by a mob.

Everywhere Paul went, two things happened. One, he

preached the truth of Jesus Christ and people got saved. Two, he got into trouble for preaching about Jesus Christ. That was just Paul. He was a bigmouth for Jesus. He didn't care what people thought about him. He just wanted to get the message out about Jesus. And he did.

Paul couldn't be stopped. One time, some people threw rocks at him. His friends thought Paul had been killed. But after they dragged his body out of town, he got up, dusted himself off, and went back into the town to preach some more!

EXPECT THE UNEXPECTED

Persecution is what happens when God's enemies try to stop His plans. But God can use that persecution to actually make His plans happen. It doesn't always make sense, but it's true. Think of Jesus: When He was killed on the cross, Satan thought he had stopped God's plan of salvation. But it was actually part of God's plan! Because Jesus died, anyone who believes in Him can be saved. So if you're being persecuted for your faith in Jesus, know that it's all part of God's plan for your life.

Paul's Second Missionary Journey (Acts 15–18)

For Paul's second missionary journey, God led him and his team to the city of Philippi in Macedonia. As usual, Paul and his buddy Silas got arrested, this time for casting an evil spirit out of a slave girl. That was a good thing to do, but her masters didn't like it (read Acts 16:16-24 to see why).

In their prison cell, Paul and Silas sang worship songs late into the night. Suddenly, an earthquake shook the door open and their chains fell off! Because of this awesome event, the jailer and his whole family came to believe in Jesus.

Paul's Third Missionary Journey (Acts 18—20)

On Paul's third missionary journey, he stayed in a city called Ephesus for about three years. Paul preached the gospel and people came to Christ—and of course, Paul got in trouble for it. At one point, a riot broke out after Paul preached, so he left for Greece and stayed there for a while.

Paul's Road to Rome (Acts 20—28)

Then Paul returned to Jerusalem even though the Holy Spirit told him that he would be arrested there. Sure enough, the Jewish leaders arrested him and beat him. They hated that Paul had become a Christian. Then some Roman guards came and took Paul away.

That night, God told Paul, "Be encouraged, Paul. Just as you have been a witness to me here in Jerusalem, you must preach the Good News in Rome as well" (Acts 23:11). It was part of God's plan for Paul to be arrested. That's because he would be sent to Rome, the capital city of the whole empire, where the gospel could spread farther and faster.

After waiting two years for his trial, Paul told the Roman governor that he wanted to tell his side of the story to the emperor. So the governor sent Paul from Jerusalem to Rome.

In Rome, Paul lived in a house while he waited for his trial. He was chained to a guard all the time. But that meant he could talk to them about Jesus—and they couldn't go anywhere! Paul also got to tell the local Jews about Jesus. And he wrote many letters to different churches, some of which we'll look at later in this book.

Acts doesn't tell us what happened to Paul after that. But that's okay because the book of Acts isn't really his story. It's the Holy Spirit's story. The Holy Spirit came and started the church. He gave the believers power and courage to share the truth about Jesus. He told them where to go, who to talk to, and what to say. That's His job.

And the Holy Spirit is still doing His job today. Jesus is still working through His people. You and I are part of what Peter, Paul, and the apostles began and what many others have continued through the centuries.

TOUR GUIDE

- The Holy Spirit filled me and helped me speak boldly about Jesus.
- I was the first martyr in the church (that is, the first person killed for my faith in Christ).
- Like Jesus, I forgave the people who killed me.
- Read Acts 7:51-60 to find out who I am.

Enjoy Your Trip

Asking the Right Questions

When Saul became a Christian, he asked two important questions: "Who are You, Lord?" and "What do You want me to do?" (see Acts 9:1-6). The Bible answers the first question: Jesus is the Lord, the Son of God, and the Savior of the world. Once you accept that and give your life to Him, you can ask the second question. There are some things God wants every Christian to do, like obey His Word. But when it comes to details, God will guide you. For example, as you try to decide what you should do when you grow up, the Lord will help you find your role in His greater plan.

Where's the Gospel?

Luke said that he only wrote about what Jesus "began to do and teach" (Acts 1:1). That word *began* is really important. The Gospels explain who Jesus was and what He did during His earthly ministry, but that was just the *beginning* of the story. Jesus didn't stop working when He went back into heaven. He told His apostles to continue His work and tell people about God's good news of salvation. The Holy Spirit helps us continue that work today.

ROMANS

Check Your Location

The apostle Paul wrote the book of Romans during the first years of Emperor Nero's reign. Nero didn't like Christians. He persecuted the early church, arresting and even killing many believers. Paul knew the believers in Rome needed to understand the basics of their beliefs so they could hold tightly to their faith. So in his letter to them, he explained almost every major teaching in Christianity. We'll look at Romans in four sections: God's wrath, God's grace, God's plan, and God's will.

Plot Your Course

The Wrath of God (Romans 1–3)

To Paul, there were only two groups of people in the world: saints and ain'ts! The *saints* are believers and the *ain'ts* are unbelievers. The *ain'ts* include people who have no faith at all, people who think doing nice things will save them, and people who think keeping religious rules will save them. Paul made it clear that none of the *ain'ts* meet God's requirements for being holy. That means God can judge them.

Unbelievers can't make the excuse of not knowing God is real. Our universe shows just how real He is! And God has put the knowledge that He is real deep inside all our hearts. But many people still ignore Him. The consequences of doing that are terrifying and last forever. That's why Paul didn't hold back with the truth.

And the truth is that God is holy. That means He can't stand sin. He may put up with it for a long time. But if we don't do something about our sin *before* we die, we will experience His wrath over our sin *after* we die.

But what can we do? Following all the laws in the Old Testament won't save us and get us to heaven. Paul said those laws just show us how sinful we are: "Everyone has sinned; we all fall short of God's glorious standard" (Romans 3:23).

No one can ever be good enough to get to heaven on their own. That's the bad news.

The Grace of God (Romans 3–8)

But here's the good news: We don't have to be good enough. Paul said, "We are made right with God by placing our faith in Jesus Christ" (Romans 3:22). Just think of that. Your sins can be forgiven and you can be made right with God. You just have to trust that Jesus died to save you.

God doesn't save us because we've done a lot of good things. He saves us because He loves us and gives us *grace*. Grace means getting something good that you don't deserve. Jesus took the bad news (our sin) when He died on the cross so we could get the good news of salvation. That's a great deal!

When we sin, we get paid back with death. We are dead spiritually, and we are cut off from God. But God wants to fix that. He offers us a free gift: "eternal life through Christ Jesus our Lord" (Romans 6:23). That free gift is the grace of God!

Once you have this gift, you also get God's power to live. You don't have to do what everyone else around you is doing. You only have to do what pleases God. And the Holy Spirit helps you do that every day.

God's grace also means that "all that happens to us is working for our good if we love God and are fitting into his plans" (Romans 8:28 TLB). No matter what happens, good or bad, you are God's. Nothing can separate you from His love! Once you are His, there's no changing it. Wrap that truth around you like a warm blanket on a chilly night.

The Plan of God (Romans 9—11)

After wrapping us up in the comfort of God's grace, Paul turned to God's plans for us. When you follow Jesus, you have to live it out in your everyday life. The way that Jesus loves you should be the pattern for how you love others. That means being kind, respectful, and truthful to everyone.

God's plan of salvation is for *anyone* who accepts Jesus as Lord and Savior. "Anyone who calls upon the name of the Lord will be saved" (Romans 10:13 TLB). It doesn't matter who we are or what we've done. We can all be saved. But the first step is to admit our sin and realize we need to be saved from it. That's when we can ask Jesus to save us. And He will!

The Will of God (Romans 12—15)

In the last part of Romans, Paul talked about how to know God's will for our lives and live as followers of Jesus.

Paul said, "I plead with you to give your bodies to God because of all he has done for you" (Romans 12:1). Giving God your body sounds like some kind of sacrifice, doesn't it? That's because it is.

Paul was saying if Jesus is truly your Lord and Savior, you should willingly offer Him your whole life. You don't do that because it will save you. You do it because you love Him and want to serve Him with all of yourself.

How do you do that? You think of others' needs before you think of your needs. You look out for those who can't look out for themselves. You read the Bible so you can know what God wants you to do, and then you do it. You pray regularly, asking God for help and thanking Him for all He has done for you.

Paul also said, "Don't copy the behavior and customs of this world, but let God transform you into a new person by changing the way you think. Then you will learn to know God's will for you, which is good and pleasing and perfect" (verse 2).

Let God *transform* you. *Transform* just means *change*. Think of it like this: Before you came to know Jesus, you were just a caterpillar, a tiny creepy-crawly. But when you decided to follow Jesus, He put you in a cocoon.

The cocoon is where you learn to follow Jesus and start to change. When He is done working on you, you will emerge from the cocoon as a new creature: a beautiful butterfly. Then you'll soar above the world and its ways. But it takes time to be transformed. So keep trusting God and be patient.

Enjoy Your Trip

Where's the Gospel?

Paul wrote Romans so we could understand the truth and power of the gospel. That's why he focused on the most important thing about the gospel: God's righteousness came through Jesus Christ. *Righteousness* means thinking and doing the right things in God's eyes. We can't be righteous without God's help. We can never *be* good enough or *do* enough good deeds to gain salvation. But because Jesus Christ came and died on the cross for our sins, we can be *made* right with God. That happens simply through our faith in Him. That's why the gospel is such good news!

▶ Don't Cause Others to Stumble

Read about a better alternative—living in harmony—in Romans 14:13-22.

1 AND 2 CORINTHIANS

Check Your Location

The apostle Paul wrote two letters to the church in Corinth. These letters are called 1 Corinthians and 2 Corinthians. The church there had a big problem. Many Christian believers were doing the same bad things as the nonbelievers around them. They wanted to be like everyone else more than they wanted to be like Jesus. They behaved selfishly and disobeyed Jesus's commands to love one another. So Paul wrote and told them to shape up!

Sometime after Paul wrote 1 Corinthians, false teachers came along and said bad things about Paul. So Paul set the record straight. In Paul's second letter to the Corinthians, he spoke more about himself than in any of his other letters. He wasn't trying to brag about himself but about Jesus. He talked about his ministry and encouraged the Corinthians to stick to the truth of the gospel.

1 CORINTHIANS

Plot Your Course

A Church Divided (1 Corinthians 1)

The first thing Paul talked to the Corinthian church about was a lack of unity. These Christians were taking sides, acting like their favorite teacher was the only one worth following.

As a result, cliques were forming in the church and dividing people. Paul reminded them that Jesus wants the church to be unified and to support one another. The good news of Jesus Christ is for *everyone*.

Paul said, "God chose things the world considers foolish in order to shame those who think they are wise" (1 Corinthians 1:27). I love that verse! God uses regular, everyday people to show off His glory.

Growing Up in the Spirit (1 Corinthians 2–4)

Next, Paul told the Corinthians that they needed to grow up spiritually. Paul loved to see people come to Christ, but being "born again" is just the first step. Like a baby learning to walk and talk, you still have to grow as a believer.

That means learning about God and how He wants you to live. You have to trust Him with all of your thoughts. And you have to replace your old ways of doing things with His new ways. That means no more arguing, complaining, or being selfish. Then you can mature as a Christian with the help of the Holy Spirit, our best teacher.

Dirty Thoughts Lead to Dirty Deeds (1 Corinthians 5–7)

The city of Corinth was a bad place. Most people did whatever they wanted, especially when it came to sex. This sexual sin started creeping into the church too. And no one was saying or doing anything about it!

The Corinthian believers thought they were being open-minded by not saying anything about this bad behavior. But Paul said they should have been crying about it! There are times when we should show grace. But other times, we have to stand up for God's truth. And we should be sad—not angry or judgmental—when people aren't following God's truth.

If you have received Jesus as your Lord and Savior, the Holy Spirit is living inside you. So keep your mind and body pure.

Freedom, Truth, and Love (1 Corinthians 8—16)

Jesus wants us to put God first, others second, and ourselves last. It's good to read the Bible and learn a lot about God. But we should use what we learn to love others. Paul said, "Although being a 'know-it-all' makes us feel important, what is really needed to build the church is love" (1 Corinthians 8:1 TLB).

Remember, no one in the church is perfect. God knows this, and He still loves us. Because of that, we need to love other believers even when we don't like the way they're acting. We need to build one another up, not put one another down. Because of Jesus, we are free to do the right thing. He gives us the power to do it.

God has given you a lot of freedom to do what you want. But everything you do matters to Him: who your friends are, how you act at church and school, what shows and videos you watch, and what music you listen to.

So whatever you do, do it in a way that shows how great you think God is. Paul said, "Whether you eat or drink, or whatever you do, do it all for the glory of God" (1 Corinthians 10:31).

LEARN THE LANGUAGE—*Love*

Read 1 Corinthians 13. This chapter is one of the greatest definitions of true Christian love. Real love goes beyond feeling all tingly and good around someone you like. Real love is all about *others*. It is patient, kind, not stuck-up or rude, loyal, hopeful, and faithful. It's the kind of love Jesus showed for us. And it's the kind of love we as the church should show God and others.

Enjoy Your Trip

Where's the Gospel?

In this letter, Paul wrote, "Christ died for our sins...He was buried, and he was raised from the dead" (1 Corinthians 15:3-4). That's the gospel in a nutshell! And the gospel gives us the power to love like God. God loved us enough to give us His very best: Jesus Christ. That means we should give our very best to love others, especially our brothers and sisters in Jesus.

2 CORINTHIANS

Plot Your Course

Paul's Encouragement (2 Corinthians 1—5)

In Paul's first letter to the Corinthians, he had to tell them to grow up in their faith. He wrote some things that weren't easy to hear. But he knew that God is faithful to use hard times (and sometimes words that are hard to hear) to make us stronger in our faith. So he wrote them another letter.

Paul wanted the Corinthians to know he was standing with them in all their troubles and wanted God's best for them.

Paul also wanted to explain his ministry to them. He worked hard to share the good news about Jesus Christ, and it wasn't easy. Paul had been attacked because of his ministry. He had been beaten up and tossed in jail because people didn't want to hear about Jesus.

"But we don't give up and quit," he said. "God never abandons us" (2 Corinthians 4:8-9 TLB). Paul knew that God was always with him, and God would be with the Christians in Corinth too. Paul also reminded the Corinthians of the reward that waited for all of them: heaven.

PACK SMART

Don't waste your suffering. As Paul shared the gospel, he went through a lot of hardship. Some of it was physical (beatings, imprisonment, shipwrecks). Some of it was personal (other Christians putting him down and trying to ruin his reputation). But Paul saw that God could use all of it to teach him patience as he spread the good news about Jesus to as many people as possible. He learned to value his suffering, and that gave him joy.

Paul's Warnings (2 Corinthians 6—8)

Some false teachers had visited the Corinthians and told lies about Paul. So Paul warned the Corinthians not to team up with people who didn't show God's love or respect His truth.

That doesn't mean you can't do things with people who aren't Christians. You will have plenty of classmates and teammates who aren't believers. You should be the best classmate and teammate you can be to them. But be careful not to let them influence you with their beliefs and ways of doing things.

Paul's Challenge (2 Corinthians 9—12)

Paul then talked about the importance of the Corinthians giving some of their money to spread God's truth and help God's people. He invited them to give generously to the church in Jerusalem, which was going through hard times.

Paul wasn't forcing them to give. But their giving would show that their love was real. And Paul reminded them that Jesus had given generously to them.

When you give with a happy heart, that makes God happy. And when you give what you can, He will make sure you have what you need.

Enjoy Your Trip

The Power of Forgiveness

When someone in the church sins, we should forgive them. That doesn't mean there won't be consequences for their sin. But it does mean that when they've dealt with the consequences, we should treat them like a fellow Christian again. When we don't forgive people, bitterness grows in our heart like a weed, and Satan can divide us (look up 2 Corinthians 2:10-11).

Where's the Gospel?

In 2 Corinthians 5:21, Paul wrote, "God made Christ, who never sinned, to be the offering for our sin, so that we could be made right with God through Christ." This verse is the key to understanding the gospel. On the cross, Jesus took all of our sin—our mistakes and failures. In return, we got His innocence and right standing in God's eyes. This is called the Great Exchange. At the cross, God treated Jesus the way we deserve to be treated. This was so He could treat us the way Jesus deserves to be treated. It seems like a bad deal for Him, but it was a great deal for us!

GALATIANS

Check Your Location

The book of Galatians is a letter Paul wrote for a group of churches in Galatia (modern-day Turkey). He wrote it because some false teachers were saying that what Jesus did on the cross wasn't enough to save someone. They taught that you also had to keep the law of Moses to be saved. That was wrong. Paul wanted to make sure believers understood that we can only be saved by putting our faith in Jesus Christ.

Plot Your Course

Paul Gets Personal (Galatians 1—4)

Even though all the churches in Galatia had learned the gospel from Paul himself, they were turning away from it. False teachers had visited them and taught that you needed to receive Jesus but also follow the rules of the law to be saved. And the believers were falling for these lies! Paul had to get personal to show them the truth.

Paul used to be big on following all the rules of the law. He was a Pharisee, one of the teachers of the Jewish law. He studied it and did his best to live by it. But keeping the rules became more important to him than loving God. Now he knew that keeping God's rules couldn't save him. For that, he needed God's grace and forgiveness, which God gave him freely in Jesus Christ.

So Paul reminded the Galatians of that important truth. He

wrote, "We know that a person is made right with God by faith in Jesus Christ, not by obeying the law" (Galatians 2:16).

Paul Gets Practical (Galatians 5–6)

Then Paul wanted the Galatians to understand how the gospel works in everyday life. He said, "Christ has made us free" (Galatians 5:1 TLB). What are we free to do? For one thing, we are free from keeping a bunch of religious rules. God gave us salvation for free because He loves us and wants us to choose to love Him back.

Some people think that means they can do whatever they want. They say, "Hey, God will forgive me for any sin. So I'll just do what I want and ask Him to forgive me later." But Paul told the Galatians that was wrong. He said, "Don't use your freedom to satisfy your sinful nature. Instead, use your freedom to serve one another in love" (verse 13).

It's not always easy to do that. Paul said we have two parts inside us that are always fighting: the flesh and the Spirit. The flesh is selfish and wants to do things that aren't right in God's eyes. But the Holy Spirit lives in every believer. He helps us love what God loves and do what God wants us to do.

PACK SMART

What does it mean to "walk in the Spirit" (Galatians 5:16 NKJV)? It means to let the Holy Spirit, who lives in every believer, guide your life. It means not doing what you want but doing what Jesus wants. He wants you to love Him and love and serve other people. When you do that, the Holy Spirit produces the "fruit of the Spirit" (verse 22 NKJV) in your life: "love, joy, peace, patience, kindness, goodness, faithfulness, gentleness, and self-control" (verses 22-23).

Enjoy Your Trip

Admit You Need Help

Before you can receive God's free gift of salvation, you have to admit you need help. No one can be good enough to earn their way to heaven. No one can make themselves clean from sin. Only Jesus can. That's why Paul called the law a curse that only Jesus can save us from. Have you asked Jesus to save you yet?

Where's the Gospel?

The law shows us that we can't carry the weight of our sin. Only Jesus can carry it. And He did carry it—at the cross. Galatians 3:13 says, "Christ has rescued us from the curse pronounced by the law. When he was hung on the cross, he took upon himself the curse for our wrongdoing." That curse crushed Him, but it couldn't keep Him in the grave. Now that He is alive again, none of us have to carry the weight of our sin anymore!

EPHESIANS

Check Your Location

The book of Ephesians is another one of Paul's letters. Paul wrote it while he was in prison in Rome for preaching the gospel. In prison, he also wrote Philippians, Colossians, and Philemon. During Paul's second missionary journey, he spent almost three years in the city of Ephesus. During his third missionary journey, he started the church there and became the first pastor. One of the big ideas Paul wrote about in Ephesians is all the ways God helps us because we are His children. He then told us how to live like we're God's kids.

Plot Your Course

Did You Know You're Rich? (Ephesians 1—3)

When we came to Jesus, God adopted us as His sons and daughters. We have the power of God to help us in our daily lives. But too often, we don't use that power.

Paul wrote that God has blessed us with "every blessing in heaven because we belong to Christ" (Ephesians 1:3 TLB). All those blessings in heaven are meant to help us live on earth! Paul then described the most important blessing God has given us: God took away our sins.

God gives us grace and kindness and wisdom. He has made us part of His family. Because He lives inside us and is our power source, we can share the gospel with others. We are brothers and sisters with every Christian on the planet. That's a big family! Spiritually speaking, you are a very rich person.

Did You Know You're Different? (Ephesians 4–6)

So what will you do with all that wealth? Paul told us "to live and act in a way worthy of those who have been chosen for such wonderful blessings as these" (Ephesians 4:1 TLB).

This means to act like Jesus did. He was humble and gentle. He put the needs of others before His own. He used His gifts and talents to help others. He is our example.

Being a Christian means you live differently than everyone in the world. The "world" doesn't mean the planet we all live on. It refers to people who reject God and live however they want. Unbelievers can't understand God's ways because they don't have His light in their hearts—they only have the darkness of sin.

But Paul told us to stop living like that. You're not part of the world anymore. You're a member of God's family, so your behavior should reflect that. That means no more sexual sin, dirty jokes, cussing, greed, putting others down, or gossiping. You used to be part of the problem, but now you are part of the solution. Don't be afraid to stick out for the right reasons.

Did You Know There's a War On? (Ephesians 6:10-24)

Standing up for God will take you right into the middle of a spiritual war. This war began a long time ago in heaven. Satan decided he wanted to take God's place and rule the universe. But there is only one God. So He kicked Satan out of heaven. Satan then became the head of the "world" system, which is all the unbelievers who stand against Jesus.

Satan couldn't defeat God, but now he attacks the people God loves. He doesn't show up at your door and say, "Boo! I'm Satan. I'm here to make your life miserable." He does tricky things on a spiritual level. He discourages you, giving you thoughts like *God doesn't love me. I'm not really saved*.

So Paul gave us instructions on how to defend ourselves from this world's biggest bully. God has given us spiritual armor so we will be safe from the enemy's attacks. But you have to put on that armor and use it (see the cartoon).

God will win this spiritual war in the end. And since you're on God's side, that means you are a winner! Don't give up. Don't run away. Prepare for battle, but also prepare for total victory.

Enjoy Your Trip

Your New Wardrobe

Here's how you live for Jesus: Replace all your old habits with new, better ones. Think of it like a change of clothes. Before you came to Jesus, you were wearing smelly old clothes that didn't fit. After you came to Jesus, He gave you a new set of clothes, clean and fresh. In your everyday life, you have to take off the old clothes (all your old habits) one piece at a time. Then you replace them with new clothes (your new ways of doing things that please God).

Where's the Gospel?

In Ephesians, Paul talked a lot about "the endless treasures available to [us] in Christ" (Ephesians 3:8 TLB). Though you can't hold these treasures in your hand like money, they are just as real. You believe in them by faith, just like you believed in Jesus to save you. These treasures include the fact that God chose you, freed you, and adopted you. Then He placed you in His new community, the church. You can look forward to eternal life and also to a wonderful spiritual life right now. How cool is that?

▶ The Armor of God

Read about winning spiritual battles in Ephesians 6:10-17.

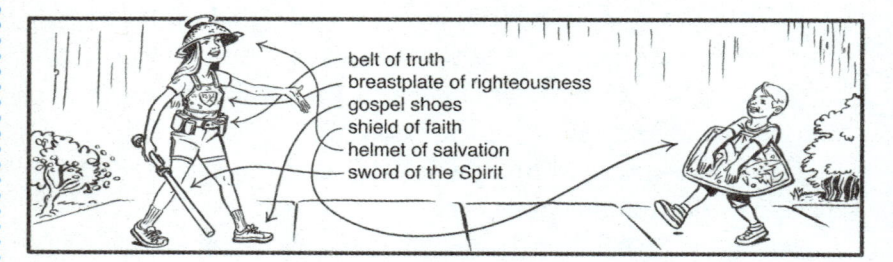

- belt of truth
- breastplate of righteousness
- gospel shoes
- shield of faith
- helmet of salvation
- sword of the Spirit

PHILIPPIANS

Check Your Location

Paul was in jail in Rome when he wrote the book of Philippians with the help of his young friend Timothy. Paul started the church in Philippi during his second missionary journey. The big idea in this letter is joy. Even though he was chained up and possibly facing his death, Paul still had joy in Jesus Christ. And Jesus was still working through Paul to bring others to faith.

Plot Your Course

Being Glad for Hard Times (Philippians 1)

Paul cared deeply about the church at Philippi. But if you look at what Paul went through in Philippi, it doesn't make a lot of sense. For starters, he didn't even want to go to Philippi. But God gave him a vision of a man telling him to come to Macedonia (the country where Philippi was). So Paul obeyed.

When he got to Philippi, he couldn't find the man from his vision. He just found a few women washing clothes by the river. To make matters worse, Paul took a serious beating and ended up in jail for preaching the gospel. That wasn't unusual for Paul, but it still wasn't much fun.

You would think Paul would say, "Philippi? I hate that place!" But instead, he told the church there, "I'm so thankful for you."

Paul was thankful because the believers in Philippi turned out to be helpful and friendly. One of the women he met at the river, Lydia, gave him a place to stay. She also became a believer in Jesus. And when Paul ended up in prison, the jailer and his family became Christians too! (Look up Acts 16:11-40 for the whole story.)

God did amazing work in Philippi even though Paul hadn't wanted to go there. When we do what God wants, some hard things might happen. But God can use it all for good purposes. Paul rejoiced for all the good that God had done in Philippi.

The Greatest Role Model (Philippians 2)

Paul then talked about his role model: Jesus Christ. He had suffered for the gospel just as Jesus had. That made him glad even though the suffering wasn't fun.

He told the Philippians about the lessons he had learned: "Don't be selfish; don't live to make a good impression on others. Be humble, thinking of others as better than yourself. Don't just think about your own affairs, but be interested in others, too, and in what they are doing" (Philippians 2:3-4 TLB). That was the attitude that Jesus had shown, and Paul wanted to be like Jesus.

Keep Pushing Forward (Philippians 3)

Paul already seemed to be a lot like Jesus! But he didn't want anyone to think he was perfect. He had a goal to reach, so he kept pushing himself forward to reach it. His goal was getting to heaven—and taking as many people as possible with him.

Peace and Joy Are the Proof of Faith (Philippians 4)

As Paul wrapped up his letter, he talked about two things that show up in a Christian's life: peace and joy. The key to having peace is to pray. Instead of worrying about *anything*, we should pray about *everything*. Then God's peace will guard us from being overwhelmed by worry.

The other thing believers need to do is rejoice. In fact, Paul commanded us to "always be full of joy in the Lord" (Philippians 4:4). Rejoicing is a command, not an option! When you don't feel like being joyful, remember that God is always good, always loving, and always there for you.

The kind of peace and joy that God gives us doesn't exist in the world. And God's peace and joy are there for you no matter what situation you're in.

Enjoy Your Trip

Hard Times Are Helpful

Being in prison and going through hard times made Paul mature as a Christian. He grew in his faith in ways he never would have if his life had been trouble-free. He learned to trust God in every situation. Even when things were hard, he still knew God could do amazing things. He said, "I can do everything through Christ, who gives me strength" (Philippians 4:13).

Where's the Gospel?

In Philippians, Paul talked about one of the most amazing parts of Jesus's character: His humility. Because Jesus is God, He could have come down to earth and bossed everyone around. But He didn't. Paul wrote that Jesus "laid aside his mighty power and glory, taking the disguise of a slave and becoming like men" (Philippians 2:7 TLB). He chose to become one of us so He could die to save us. Even though it's hard, we should humble ourselves like Jesus did and serve others. Just ask the Holy Spirit to help you be like Jesus.

COLOSSIANS

Check Your Location

Colossians is one of Paul's four letters he wrote from a Roman prison. Paul wrote to warn the believers in the city of Colossae about false teachers called the Gnostics. They taught that Jesus wasn't really a human but some kind of spirit-being that came from God. Weird, right?

So in this letter, Paul focused on who Jesus really is: both God and man. Being man meant that He could be a sacrifice for sin by shedding His blood. Being God meant that He could rise from the dead, defeating sin and death. Jesus had to be both man and God for our salvation to work. And because our salvation works, we now have the power to live our lives for Him.

Plot Your Course

The Wisdom and Power of Jesus (Colossians 1—2)

The church in Colossae had grown a lot. But growth attracts troublemakers like the Gnostics. Paul reminded the Colossians that God wanted to protect them from these false teachers. But Paul also wanted the Colossians to know God's will and have the wisdom to put it to use. How do you find out God's will? By praying, reading the Bible, and being around true believers.

And the Bible leaves no doubt who Jesus is: He is God. Specifically, He is the Son of God, the Messiah. He created the earth and everything in it. Then He came to earth to carry out God's plan to save His beloved people from the punishment of sin.

Jesus is the most one-of-a-kind person who has ever lived. He is the unique God-man. The more you know your Bible, the better you'll understand who Jesus is.

Living for Jesus (Colossians 3—4)

Jesus is the creator of everything. He holds it all together. He is also the head of the church because He defeated death and sin and saves anyone who believes in Him. Jesus is the Lord of all, and He is the only one who can be your true Savior. No one should matter more to you than Him.

So how do you live that out in your everyday life? Paul said, "Let heaven fill your thoughts; don't spend your time worrying about things down here" (Colossians 3:2 TLB). This means don't let the things you're doing or going through become more important to you than following Jesus. Bring Jesus into everything you do.

And be like Jesus. Be humble, kind, forgiving, and patient. Look out for others and do what's best for them. Avoid bad behavior, like always trying to get more stuff, lying, cussing, or speaking hateful words. If you're really living for Jesus, what you do or don't do shows it.

Enjoy Your Trip

Where's the Gospel?

Paul said, "Christ is the visible image of the invisible God" (Colossians 1:15). No one can see God the Father because He is spirit. He doesn't have a body. But God the Son (Jesus) came to earth in a human body. If you ever wondered what God is really like, just look at Jesus. And because Jesus is God, He "is first in everything" (verse 18). That means He ought to be first in our lives—in other words, the most important thing. That's the message of the gospel.

1 AND 2 THESSALONIANS

Check Your Location

The apostle Paul helped start the church in Thessalonica on his second missionary journey. He taught the believers there for about a month. Then a group of unfriendly Jews forced him to move on. After that, Paul wrote two letters to talk about the issues the Thessalonian Christians faced.

In both letters, Paul wanted the Thessalonian believers to know about God's plans for the end times and look forward to the hope of Jesus's return.

First Thessalonians is about the *rapture*. That's when Jesus will return and gather His church to meet Him in the air. Then Paul wrote 2 Thessalonians to talk about the *day of the Lord*. That's when God will bring judgment on the earth in the end times.

1 THESSALONIANS

Plot Your Course

Keep the Work Going (1 Thessalonians 1—3)

Paul was thankful for the believers in Thessalonica. He had only been their teacher for a few weeks, but they took his teaching to heart. Like Paul, they suffered for standing up for the good news of Jesus. But they handled their hard times with grace and joy. They became an example to the other churches around them.

The gospel came *to* them, and now the gospel was going out *through* them to other people. That's where the real joy of being a Christian is. It's not just when God does a work *in* you but when God does a work *through* you too.

Like a proud father, Paul rejoiced in his spiritual children's growth. He knew that they would all celebrate together in heaven someday.

Get Ready for the End (1 Thessalonians 4—5)

Paul had taught the Thessalonians about how God would judge the world at the end of time. But because of the hardships they were going through, the Thessalonians thought those end times had come! The Roman government was arresting and even killing Christians, and believers everywhere were facing lots of trouble. So Paul cleared things up for them.

Here's how the end times will work: God's final judgment will come during what's called the tribulation, the last seven years of human history. But just before the tribulation begins, Jesus will leave heaven and come into the sky above the earth. There will be a big trumpet blast and a loud shout.

Then all the believers who have died will rise from their graves and meet Jesus in the air. Jesus will make their bodies like His: whole, healthy, and glorified. After that, the rest of the believers who are alive at that time will also rise to meet Jesus in the air. We will all be transformed into our glorified bodies (look up 1 Corinthians 15:52). Then Jesus will take us home to heaven. This is what we call the rapture.

At the rapture, you'll get to be reunited with Christian friends and family members who have died before you. And you'll be with Jesus forever! That's the great hope we have as believers.

Paul gave the Thessalonian believers all this information to comfort them. The end times will be the worst time in earth's history. There will be wars, plagues, and earthquakes. That's because God will be judging the earth for rejecting His Savior, Jesus Christ. But because of the rapture, we can all breathe a sigh of relief. Anyone who is a true believer in Jesus will not be there to see it happen.

So Paul encouraged the Thessalonian believers to keep doing the good work of being faithful. They didn't know when Jesus would come back to get them and take them out of the world. So they needed to share the good news of Jesus with as many people as possible in the meantime.

Enjoy Your Trip

Where's the Gospel?

Early on in this letter, Paul talked about faith, love, and hope (look up 1 Thessalonians 1:3). In the past, you looked to Jesus to save you by *faith*. In the present, you are living in ways that show you *love* Him. In the future, you look forward with *hope* that you'll see Him again. With Jesus as your Lord and Savior, the gospel is part of every stage of your life: past, present, and future.

2 THESSALONIANS

Plot Your Course

Waiting for Christ's Return (2 Thessalonians 1)

Paul wrote 2 Thessalonians only a few months after he wrote 1 Thessalonians. The church at Thessalonica had received his letter, but they were still worried that they somehow missed the rapture. The Roman government was hunting down Christians and throwing them in jail. Some Christians were even being tortured and killed. How could this be happening?

Paul got word that the Thessalonians still had some questions—and that they wanted to know when those who were hurting them would be judged by God.

So Paul told them that God knew about their suffering and would pay back their persecutors. They might have to wait until Jesus came back for justice to be served, but it *would* be served. Jesus will return one day and bring "judgment on those who do not wish to know God and who refuse to accept his plan to save them through our Lord Jesus Christ" (verse 8 TLB). That's God's promise.

Watching Out for the Bad Guy (2 Thessalonians 2)

Then Paul told the Thessalonians about the main villain of the end times, the Antichrist. Paul didn't call him the Antichrist in this letter. He used other names for him in verse 3: "the man of lawlessness...the one who brings destruction" (NLT) and "the son of hell" (TLB).

The Antichrist will be Satan's fake version of Jesus Christ. Paul said this man will be full of satanic power and use miracles to trick anyone who doesn't belong to Jesus. Then the Antichrist will take over and try to rule the world until Jesus returns. In the end, he'll be defeated and sent to hell forever (see Revelation 19:20).

Two things have to happen before the day of the Lord begins. First there will be "a time of great rebellion against God" (2 Thessalonians 2:3 TLB). Then the Antichrist will show up.

That hadn't happened yet. So the Thessalonian believers hadn't missed the rapture. In fact, they're all waiting in heaven now for it to happen. When it does, they will return with Jesus to collect the rest of the believers from earth. Now that's something to look forward to!

Warning to Stay Busy (2 Thessalonians 3)

Knowing that God is in control of everything, including the future, might make some people lazy. There were believers in Thessalonica who felt that way. But that's not how Paul lived. He stayed busy for God and he wanted them to do the same (see 2 Thessalonians 3:10). Relaxing and having fun is okay, but we should be willing to stay busy and show as many people as we can how to get to heaven.

PACK SMART

Here is the chain of events in the end times:

- The rapture of God's people will happen.
- The last seven years of earth's history will begin (a time called the tribulation).
- Halfway through the tribulation, the Antichrist will sit in the temple and claim he is God.
- The second half of the tribulation will begin (a time called the *great* tribulation).
- At the end of the great tribulation, Jesus will return to earth with all His followers.

Enjoy Your Trip

Where's the Gospel?

Paul gave very specific details about the end times in his letters to the Thessalonians. So even though we don't know when the rapture will happen, we can trust that it is going to happen. The Bible tells us about how awful the end times are going to be. But it also tells us that God has a plan to save anyone who receives His free gift of salvation. That means when He comes back, He is coming to rescue *you*. That's worth looking forward to!

▶ **The Rapture**
Read about meeting Jesus when He returns in 1 Thessalonians 4:16-17.

1 AND 2 TIMOTHY

Check Your Location

The apostle Paul wrote two letters to his younger friend Timothy about how to be a good pastor. Timothy came to believe in Jesus because of Paul. Later, he became the pastor of the church in Ephesus. Paul had started that church and visited it on his second and third missionary journeys. The believers there held a special place in his heart—including Timothy.

Paul wrote 2 Timothy from a prison in Rome after his second arrest. It was his last letter before he was executed for his faith in Christ. Paul gave Timothy some final advice to stand strong for the faith and stand up for the truth of God's Word, no matter what.

1 TIMOTHY

Plot Your Course

Pursuing Truth for the Church (1 Timothy 1)

Timothy faced many challenges as a pastor. He had to stand up against false teaching. He had to teach God's Word well. He had to make sure other leaders in the church were true believers in Jesus. Paul didn't want his young friend to be overwhelmed by his duties, so he told Timothy how to keep his eyes on God.

First, Paul encouraged Timothy to stay in Ephesus and teach

only the truth that God has given humankind: the Bible. At that time, this included not only the Old Testament but also a new set of books and letters we now know as the New Testament.

If Timothy stuck to God's truth, he would be able to stand up to false teachers. These people taught things that God didn't say. They twisted scriptures to match their own ideas about God and Jesus. Paul warned Timothy that taking on these false teachers would be a battle. But fighting for the truth is always worth it.

Praying to Build the Church (1 Timothy 2)

Paul then told Timothy about the most important tool Timothy had: prayer. Timothy needed to be praying all the time for everyone he met, especially Roman leaders. These leaders had been rough on Christians, but praying for them meant that believers could live peaceful, godly lives.

Paul also wanted the church to pray when they came together. And when they worshipped God, there shouldn't be any distractions. Worship should always be about God, not us.

Picking Leaders for the Church (1 Timothy 3–4)

Timothy couldn't run the church by himself. He needed help from other godly men and women to do the work. So Paul told Timothy what to look for in a church leader. They must have good character and be a wholehearted follower of Jesus. They shouldn't be drunks, gossips, or greedy people. They need to represent Jesus well and do their best.

Providing Care for the Church (1 Timothy 5–6)

If church leaders do their job well, God can do great things in the church. Timothy's job was to be the example of how to treat everyone who came to church. Paul told him to respect older men and women like they were his parents. He was to treat younger men and women like they were his brothers and sisters.

Paul wanted Timothy to focus on what God wanted him to do. That was more valuable than trying to make money or make a name for himself. God would help him succeed in ways that really mattered.

PACK SMART

Money isn't the root of all evil. But the *love* of money is a root of *all kinds* of evil (see 1 Timothy 6:9-10). If making money and having things is the most important goal in your life, you will never be truly happy. Real riches are found in relationships—with Jesus and with others.

Enjoy Your Trip

Where's the Gospel?

Paul told Timothy that God "wants everyone to be saved and to understand the truth. For, there is one God and one Mediator who can reconcile God and humanity—the man Christ Jesus. He gave his life to purchase freedom for everyone" (1 Timothy 2:4-6). These verses are perfect for sharing the gospel! They say it all: God loves us and wants to save us. So He sent Jesus, who died so we could be free. It's as simple as that!

2 TIMOTHY

Plot Your Course

Stand Up for the Faith (2 Timothy 1)

Paul had spent a long time in jail, writing letters to the churches and giving good advice about how to follow Jesus.

But his time was coming to an end. Soon, the Roman government would find him guilty of being a Christian. Paul would be executed.

But Paul kept his eyes on Jesus to the end. He wrote this last letter to Timothy to tell him to stand strong for the faith.

Paul didn't want Timothy to be afraid. Between the persecution from the Roman government and Paul facing his death, Timothy had good reasons to be scared. But Paul told him, "The Holy Spirit, God's gift, does not want you to be afraid of people, but to be wise and strong" (2 Timothy 1:7 TLB). God helps us face all our fears.

Stand Up for God in All You Do (2 Timothy 2)

Paul encouraged Timothy in his job as a pastor. He gave examples from everyday life of how to live for God. Like good soldiers, we follow God's orders. Like athletes, we work hard to win a prize. Like farmers, we get paid for bringing in a good crop. And like workers, we want to be proud of doing a good job.

All of these examples have one thing in common: determination. Being a godly person takes hard work as you study the Bible and prepare for life's challenges.

Stand Up to the World (2 Timothy 3)

Paul gave Timothy a list of problems believers face. People love themselves and money more than they love God. They make fun of God and those who follow Him. They disrespect their parents and put others down. They're mean and hate what is good. They betray their friends. Some act religious but still reject God's truth.

Paul told Timothy to stay away from people like that. Instead, Timothy needed to stick to the truth of the Bible so he could stand up to the world. Paul said that God gives the Bible its power. That's why it can tell us what's wrong and right in our lives (see 2 Timothy 3:16).

> **LEARN THE LANGUAGE—*Doctrine***
> In this letter, Paul talked to Timothy about following "doctrine." It's a serious word, but don't be afraid of it. It just means Bible teaching that sticks to the truth of God's Word. True doctrine will keep you standing strong in hard times.

Stand Up Until the End (2 Timothy 4)

Paul sensed that his time was short. He told his young friend to keep fighting for God's truth and doing what was right until the end, just as Paul himself had done.

Not long after Paul wrote this letter, Emperor Nero ordered that he be killed. So Paul was beheaded in Rome. He left the world behind and went to be with Jesus in heaven, receiving his reward for a life well lived. Paul wanted Timothy to receive the same reward when his life was done, and I'm sure he would want the same for us.

Enjoy Your Trip

Where's the Gospel?

Paul's life was all about the gospel. The gospel is good news! God doesn't want to see us go to hell when we die. He wants us to have a life with Him in heaven—*forever*. The only way to get that is to make Jesus Christ your Lord and Savior. That's the message Paul lived and died for. We should follow his example.

TITUS AND PHILEMON

Check Your Location

In the book of Titus, Paul wrote to his friend Titus, who was the pastor of the church in Crete. Crete is an island in the Mediterranean Sea near Greece. Paul gave Titus advice about how to run the church there.

The book of Philemon is a short letter that Paul wrote from a prison in Rome. It's different from Paul's other letters because it's a personal letter. He wrote it to a man named Philemon about one of Philemon's slaves who had run away. Paul wanted Philemon to make things right with his slave, showing God's love and mercy to a new brother in Christ.

TITUS

Plot Your Course

The Right Man for the Job (Titus 1)

Titus was a Gentile (that means he wasn't Jewish). He became a Christian because Paul told him about how Jesus came to save everyone, not just Jews. Titus went with Paul on his third missionary journey. He was also at an important meeting of church leaders in Jerusalem (see Acts 15). Leading a growing church can be hard, but Paul knew Titus was the right man for the job in Crete.

Every good leader needs great helpers. Just like Paul had told Timothy, Paul told Titus to pick strong leaders for the church. These leaders needed to have good character, obey God, live by the Bible, and help Titus stand up to false teachers.

The Right Teaching for the Church (Titus 2)

One of the most important jobs Titus did was disciple other believers. To disciple means to teach. Titus taught the men and women in the church at Crete to follow Jesus. Paul encouraged Titus to "promote the kind of living that reflects wholesome teaching" (Titus 2:1). He wanted to make sure Titus was preparing them to live godly lives. This was so they would look forward to and be ready for Jesus to return—just like we should be!

The Right Example to the World (Titus 3)

Paul told the church in Crete to follow the pattern that all good churches follow. We start by following solid leaders. They faithfully teach us God's truth and help us live it out in our lives. Once that happens, we take the next step: We represent God to the world.

Christians should be good and obedient citizens, neighbors, workers, and students. We should do our best to get along with everyone we meet. And above all, we should follow Jesus's example by serving others and helping them in life. This will really get their attention. Then people will be more likely to listen to us when we talk about Jesus, and we'll have a chance to win them over with the gospel.

Enjoy Your Trip

Where's the Gospel?

Paul told Titus a short version of the gospel (read Titus 2:11-13). This is the gospel in a nutshell: We needed saving from sin, God sent Jesus to save us from our sin, and now we live for the Lord as we look forward to when Jesus comes again.

PHILEMON

Plot Your Course

A Slave Who Was Free at Last (Philemon 1–21)

Philemon was a leader of the church at Colossae. He had a good reputation as a believer. Paul wrote to him about Philemon's slave, Onesimus. It was normal for Roman citizens to own slaves. Onesimus had wronged Philemon in some way, and then he ran away.

While he was on the run, Onesimus had met Paul. Paul helped him choose Jesus as his Lord and Savior. The slave who fled from serving Philemon found freedom from sin in Christ!

Paul wanted to encourage Philemon to do the right thing as a Christian. So he asked Philemon to take Onesimus back and treat him fairly. Onesimus and Philemon were now brothers because they were both believers. In God's eyes, slaves and their owners were equals. They went to church, worshipped, and learned about God's Word together.

Paul wasn't telling Philemon he had to set Onesimus free. That wasn't what Roman law required. Philemon could set Onesimus free if he wanted to. But Paul just wanted Philemon to take Onesimus back and give him another chance to work for him. If Philemon didn't, Onesimus would be in big trouble. Runaway slaves were usually sentenced to hard labor or even death.

As Christians, we all stand on equal footing with each other (look up Galatians 3:28). And we can all do what's needed to make things right. Onesimus could apologize and ask Philemon to forgive him. He could promise he would be a good worker. And Philemon could forgive Onesimus and treat him fairly.

Paul wanted them to enjoy a deeper relationship as spiritual brothers. He told Philemon, "Perhaps you could think of it this way: that he ran away from you for a little while so that now he can be yours forever, no longer only a slave, but something much better—a beloved brother" (verses 15-16 TLB).

Paul was looking at the big picture: God's picture. Onesimus broke the law and ran away, but God led him to Paul, who led him to Jesus. Coming to Christ is the most important thing you can ever do in life! And it should change the way you look at others.

Paul reminded Philemon that all of us were once slaves to sin. We all owe Jesus something we can never repay. If we are thankful for Jesus and His gift of salvation, we should show it by how we treat others—especially when it's not easy to do.

Enjoy Your Trip

Where's the Gospel?

This letter shows the love and mercy of Jesus Christ in action. Paul offered to pay Philemon any debts Onesimus owed him so that they could make peace and have a good relationship. That's a beautiful picture of what Jesus has done for us. On the cross, Jesus paid what we owed God: the cost of sin's wages, which is death. We were slaves of sin, but He paid to set us free so we could have a right relationship with God.

HEBREWS

Check Your Location

The Old Testament is full of prophecies about the Messiah. The book of Hebrews is about how Jesus fulfilled all of them. His death was God's greatest triumph. It's also about how much better Jesus is than anything or anyone else! We actually don't know who wrote the book of Hebrews. It's a mystery. Whoever it was knew a lot about Judaism and the Old Testament, especially the book of Leviticus. And whoever it was really wanted Jewish believers to continue to follow Jesus Christ. The goal of the book was to get Jewish unbelievers to choose to follow Him.

Plot Your Course

Jesus Is Better (Hebrews 1—10)

Right away, the writer of Hebrews began telling us all about why Jesus is better than anything and anyone else. Here are some of the main points he made in this book.

- Jesus is better than angels and prophets. God sent angels from heaven and He also used prophets to speak to people. But Jesus *is* God. Jesus said all that God ever wanted to say, especially the gospel.
- Jesus is better than a priest. In the Jewish law, priests made animal sacrifices to pay the cost of the people's

sin. But when Jesus sacrificed Himself, He paid the price of sin once and for all. He was both the perfect sacrifice for sin and the perfect priest to offer it.

- Jesus brought in a better covenant—the new covenant. The old covenant required that you keep the law perfectly. But nobody could do that, even though many tried to. In the new covenant that Jesus made, all you have to do is believe in Him. Then you'll keep His rules because you love Him. And you'll have His power to help you.

- Jesus is better than the tabernacle in the wilderness or the temple in Jerusalem. Those were places people went to offer a sacrifice, pray, and get close to God. But because of Jesus, you don't have to go to a sacred place to get to God. Anyone who believes can come to Him right where they are.

- Jesus is better than the old way of sacrificing. After Jesus sacrificed Himself on the cross, no more sacrifices are needed to pay sin's cost. Jesus's blood paid the full amount we owe.

Christians Should Live Better (Hebrews 11–13)

After the writer of Hebrews said all that, he explained how we should live because of everything Jesus has done. The biggest thing we should do is live by faith. Here is why faith is so important: The rituals of the Old Testament were like a stain remover that stopped working after a few hours. They couldn't really clean sin away once and for all. But the sacrifice of Jesus can. You just have to put your faith in Him.

What exactly is faith? "It is the confident assurance that something we want is going to happen. It is the certainty that what we hope for is waiting for us, even though we cannot see it up ahead" (Hebrews 11:1 TLB). Biblical faith is more than a positive attitude or wishful thinking. It's based on evidence that God is who He says He is and keeps all His promises.

Then the author of Hebrews listed people who lived by faith and trusted God by obeying what He said to do: Noah, Abraham, Sarah, Isaac, Jacob, Joseph, Moses, and David.

We have so many great examples of faith to follow. The people in the Bible we think of as heroes were just regular people. What made them amazing was their faith in God. These were just ordinary people who trusted in an extraordinary God. They kept their eyes on God through all of life's good and bad times.

So let's follow their example, running the race of life by keeping our eyes on Jesus. That means being patient in hard times and in persecution. It also means loving other believers and looking forward to the hope of heaven.

Because of who Jesus is as God, because of His perfect life, and because of what He did on the cross, Jesus is by far the best. No one and nothing else comes anywhere close to Him!

Enjoy Your Trip

Where's the Gospel?

The gospel is on every page of Hebrews. One way the writer of Hebrews described Jesus was as our great High Priest. As our High Priest, Jesus brought us and God together by His perfect sacrifice on the cross. That means we don't have to be scared to talk to God or worry that He'll be mad at us because of our imperfect life. We can be confident when we come to Him and ask for His help. Through Jesus's death and resurrection, He built an unbreakable bridge between us and God. How cool is that?

▶ The Hall of Faith

Read about Noah, Sarah, Joseph, and others in Hebrews 11.

JAMES

Check Your Location

This book was written by James, a leader of the early church and the half brother of Jesus. (Can you imagine having Jesus as your older brother?) This book is sort of like the book of Proverbs. It's filled with wisdom about living well. James made a very important point in his book: If your faith in Jesus is real, you'll show it by obeying what the Bible says. James then gave lots of practical instructions on how you can do that.

Plot Your Course

James's book is like a manual on how to become a mature Christian. There are five big points he made about how to be a strong believer:

Be Patient in Trials (James 1)

First, James told us to be joyful when we go through hard times. That sounds really hard to do, right? But the reason is that trials help you grow in patience and faith. When you don't know how to deal with a hardship or temptation, ask God how to handle it. He'll give you the wisdom you need!

Live What You Believe (James 2)

A mature Christian doesn't just talk about their faith—they live it out. Anyone can say they believe there's a God, but James said even demons believe that! Real faith shows itself by how a person lives their life. You don't just believe it in your mind—you also show it with your actions.

That doesn't mean you do good things in order to save yourself. You're already saved if you believe in Jesus and trust in His sacrifice on the cross. Doing good works is a response to being saved. It shows that your faith is alive and real.

Watch What You Say (James 3)

Mature Christians are also careful about what they say. They keep their tongue under control and make their words count for good. That's because words are powerful! With your words, you can spread rumors, lie, call someone else names, curse, and more. The tongue can destroy.

Only by asking God for wisdom can we learn how to use our tongue for good things, like building others up and praising the Lord.

Be Humble (James 4)

Sometimes people just don't get along—even in the church. But a mature Christian deals with conflict the right way: by listening, thinking carefully, and not reacting in anger.

We also need to follow Jesus's example of being humble and let the Lord run our lives. That's a good thing because James said God gives grace to those who are humble.

Make Your Trials Count (James 5)

Finally, James told believers to trust God with their lives and hang in there through hard times. Mature Christians keep pushing on because they have hope that Jesus will return and make things right one day. Until then, the Lord will strengthen believers as they trust Him, pray, forgive others, and spread the gospel.

Enjoy Your Trip

Growth Spurt!

Growing as a Christian isn't something that happens overnight. It happens throughout your whole life, starting right now! You grow when you choose to obey God's Word. James said that obeying the Bible proves you love God and have faith in Him. Do you do what the Bible tells you to do? What does this say about your faith—is it the real deal?

Where's the Gospel?

We should rejoice in the Lord when we go through hard times. That's because, as James said, suffering makes you grow as a Christian. Trials are a way we can become more like Jesus, who went through ultimate suffering on the cross. So when you're going through a tough time, try praying, "Lord, how can I become more like Jesus because of this?"

▶ Faith That Works

Read about a living faith in James 2:14-17.

1 AND 2 PETER

Check Your Location

Peter the apostle was one of Jesus's best friends when Jesus was on the earth. That didn't mean Peter was perfect! But God took him and turned him into a solid leader of the early church. He wrote a pair of letters to Christians who were going through terrible persecution from the Roman government.

In 1 Peter, Peter encouraged believers to honor God in how they lived. In 2 Peter, he warned them about false teachers. In both letters, he encouraged Christians to be bold and stand up for the truth.

1 PETER

Plot Your Course

Take Comfort—You're Saved! (1 Peter 1–5)

Peter wrote to a group of Christians who were being mistreated and persecuted for their faith in Jesus. They were getting weary and discouraged. He wanted to remind them that God was with them, especially in such hard times.

Like with all believers, God chose them to be His before the universe was even made. That meant He would be with them on earth and He would also get them safely to heaven. Their salvation was certain! So Peter encouraged them to stay strong, trust God, and commit themselves to follow His plans.

In the meantime, they needed to represent Christ well—just as we need to do today. We need to be holy in everything we do, focusing on God and not on the things of this world.

We also need to grow in our relationship with Jesus. You're not supposed to accept Jesus as your Savior and then live however you want. You need to follow Him by learning His Word, the Bible, and doing what it says.

Then unbelievers will see that you live differently from them. Sometimes that means you'll be made fun of or even hurt for following Jesus. But when you suffer for doing the right thing, Peter said that's a very good thing! You're following Jesus's example, and it brings you closer to God.

Peter ended his letter by telling all the members of the church to love and serve one another. Together, they would be able to stand up to persecution from the world and bring glory to God.

Enjoy Your Trip

Where's the Gospel?

Even if you're a Christian, God still sometimes lets you suffer. But He uses that suffering for your good. Peter wrote, "It is no shame to suffer for being a Christian. Praise God for the privilege of being in Christ's family and being called by his wonderful name!" (1 Peter 4:16 TLB). Just think of the gospel. Because Jesus went through the horrible pain of dying on the cross, He brought about the greatest good in all of history: salvation for the world! If you're His, He will watch over you and give you strength.

2 PETER

Plot Your Course

The Fortress of Truth (2 Peter 1–3)

The church is like a fortress of truth in this world. Our enemy, Satan, wants to attack it by using false teachers (also called false prophets) to spread lies. These people can make it confusing to follow Jesus.

Peter wrote this letter so Christians would know how to spot a fake. Once false teachers have been identified, they should be kicked out of the church. That may sound harsh, but it's like a doctor removing cancer from the body.

False teachers say things that can sound good when you first hear them, but they take a little bit of truth and mix in a sneaky lie. For example, they say you don't really have to believe in Jesus to get to heaven. That's a seriously wrong teaching! And it can affect where someone ends up spending eternity: heaven or hell.

That's why the truth is so important. And that's why we have to know God's truth in the first place. The good news is God has given us everything we need to know His truth and live a godly life. It's all found in the Bible. We all have a responsibility to learn the Bible, live it out, and fight for it. That's what I hope this book can help you do!

The believers Peter wrote to wondered when God was finally going to step in and stop these false teachers. Peter reminded them that one day Jesus will come back and judge these teachers—and the whole world. In fact, Jesus will destroy the earth in the end. Then He will make a brand new one—without all those who reject Him and His truth. Sin and evil will be gone forever!

Even when it feels like God is taking a long time to do something about all the bad stuff in the world, we can trust that He will do something. One day, He will judge false teachers and the people who follow their teachings. But He's being patient for now because He wants to give everyone the chance to be saved by accepting Jesus as their Savior.

When we stand up to false teachers, you and I can make sure people have the chance to do just that.

PACK SMART

Don't be fooled by someone who only looks like a Christian on the outside. Peter gave us three ways to tell if someone is a teacher of God's truth:

- Character: Look up Galatians 5:22-23. Does this person show the fruit of the Spirit in their life?
- Creed: *Creed* means *belief*. Does this person believe Jesus is the only way to heaven?
- Converts: Look at the people who follow this person's teaching. Do they also show the fruit of the Spirit in their lives?

Enjoy Your Trip

Where's the Gospel?

A popular false teaching today is called the health-and-wealth gospel. This teaching says that God will give you whatever you need to be healthy, rich, and happy. But that's not always true! In fact, Jesus said we would have troubles in this life. The true gospel doesn't promise that you'll have a carefree life, but it does promise that when you die, you'll go to heaven. I'd take an incredible eternity over an easy life on earth any day!

1, 2, AND 3 JOHN AND JUDE

Check Your Location

Jesus's good friend and follower John probably wrote 1 John, 2 John, and 3 John. John was nicknamed "the Apostle of Love" because of how much he used the word *love* in his books. John had a long and fruitful life as a leader of the early church. He wrote these letters to encourage Christians to keep believing in Jesus. If we love Jesus, we should love the truth and live it out.

Jude might have been one of Jesus's twelve disciples—or even His half brother! In his letter, Jude spoke up against some popular but wrong teachings being taught in the early church. He wanted the church to stand strong and fight against what wasn't the truth. Why? Because the truth is worth fighting for!

1 JOHN

Plot Your Course

John's first letter looks at five big topics about how we should live because we believe in Jesus.

Be Friendly

John talked about *fellowship* in this letter. Fellowship means having friendships with other believers based on the big thing we have in common: Jesus Christ. When we have fellowship with other believers and truly love them, that means we really know and follow Jesus.

Be Holy

Following Jesus means you should no longer follow the world and its ways of doing things. That doesn't mean you won't make mistakes. But as you follow Jesus, He'll make you more and more like Him. That's what being holy means. You start to be like Jesus in how you think, talk, and act.

Be Happy

Believing in Jesus gives us joy. Joy isn't putting on a fake smile or pretending to be happy in order to look like a good Christian. Joy comes from being forgiven by God and living a love-filled life. And joy is the real sign that God is part of your life. True happiness comes from Him alone.

Be on Your Guard

John reminded believers that we have a duty to stand for God's truth. He warned the early church about the false teaching of the Gnostics. They were a mystical group that thought they knew more about Jesus than the apostles. But God has given us all the tools we need to tell the truth from the lies.

The biggest truth detector we have is what people say about Jesus Christ. If they believe He is God's Son who came to die on the cross and save us from our sins, then you know they belong to God. Also, make sure they believe in and follow the rest of what the Bible says.

Be Sure

John said there are several ways you can know if you really belong to Jesus: Are you living like it? Do you obey God's Word and live how He tells you to live? Do you believe in God's truth? Do you love other believers? If these things describe your life, then you're His!

Enjoy Your Trip

Where's the Gospel?

Following Jesus means rejecting the world's way of thinking and living. Once you're saved, you live it out in your thoughts, words, and actions. And as you learn God's truth and put it into practice, your life will be changed. Now *that's* good news!

2 JOHN

Plot Your Course

Real Love Requires Real Truth (2 John 1–13)

John's big theme in this little letter is being a lover of the truth. John encouraged Christians to be careful about how they love other people. We need to make sure that we're always standing up for the truth and being careful about who we let teach in the church.

John told Christians to love one another. Then he said, "Love means doing what God has commanded us" (2 John 6). This means we need to follow God's truth while we love others.

Christians should be known for the way we love. But your love needs boundaries, like a fence around your yard. Having boundaries means you have to speak up when you see sin in someone's life. You need to find the kindest, gentlest way to do it, but you should still do it.

The world usually believes that loving someone means you never speak out against their choices or beliefs. But sometimes you have to, especially as a Christian! If you don't, then that person might never learn the truth of the gospel.

Love and truth should always go hand in hand. In this letter, John was worried that some Christians weren't sticking to the truth. If they weren't, false teachers could sneak into the church and teach whatever they wanted. So John said that if a preacher didn't preach the truth of Christ, believers shouldn't welcome him. They needed to keep false teachers from spreading their lies.

Enjoy Your Trip

Where's the Gospel?

Jesus loved everyone, but He also told everyone the truth. A lot of people didn't like that. He laid down His life in love so that we could be saved from our sin. But that sacrifice was necessary in the first place because we are sinful beings! So there are two sides to the gospel, truth and love: (1) The *truth* is that we sin and need to be saved, and (2) Jesus *loved* us enough to die for our sins and save us.

3 JOHN

Plot Your Course

Living by the Truth (3 John 1–14)

Third John is the shortest book in the Bible. In it, John pointed out three different individuals in the early church. Two of these guys were great examples of how to live out God's truth by loving others. But the third guy was bad news.

John was happy to hear that Gaius, the man he wrote this letter to, was living out the truth. That's not an easy thing to do. Our world doesn't accept what God and the Bible say is true. They think as long as you're sincere about whatever you believe, you'll go to heaven. But all roads don't lead to God any more than they do to New York City. So John praised Gaius for believing God's truth and living it out every day. John also mentioned Demetrius, another believer who was living out the truth.

On the other hand, there was a man in the church named Diotrephes. He was a bad example. Diotrephes was selfish and wanted to be a big shot. He even spoke out against John. Diotrephes was not showing his love for the truth—if you love the truth, then you'll love other people who also love the truth. So John called him out on it.

Enjoy Your Trip

Where's the Gospel?

In the early church, false prophets came right to your door, selling lies. But John told believers only to receive teachers of the truth into their homes. Be on guard against those who would lead us away from the true gospel. The best way to do that is to know the true gospel and learn God's truth by reading the Bible.

JUDE

Plot Your Course

Defending the Faith (Jude 1–25)

Jude wrote his book to take a stand against *apostasy*, which is a word that means to turn away from Jesus Christ. When someone does that, it's usually because they have changed something in the true gospel.

Jude knew the church needed to stick to the truth of the gospel, so he wrote very strongly against the false things some people were teaching as truth. He called Christians to "contend earnestly for the faith" (Jude 3 NKJV). To "contend earnestly" means to put up a good fight. All Christians should defend the truth of their faith.

So Jude told believers to stay active in the truth and build up our faith. How do you build your faith? You pray, you hang around other Christians, you read God's Word, and you follow what He tells you to do.

Jude also told Christians to help other Christians live in the truth. This means lovingly telling them when they're doing something wrong or believing something against what the Bible teaches. The early church had to fight for the truth—and we do today too!

PACK SMART

What's the best way to make sure you know what the truth is? Reading God's Word, the Bible, because it's the ultimate source of truth. We have to listen cautiously when people talk about God. Jude would tell us to be careful that we don't start believing things that are against what Scripture teaches. When and where do you read your Bible?

Enjoy Your Trip

Where's the Gospel?

Jude wrote his letter to defend the gospel. The gospel is the most important truth in the world: Jesus Christ died for the sins of the world so that we could be saved from death and hell when we believe in Him. We need to guard that truth with everything we've got.

REVELATION

Check Your Location

Revelation is one of the most incredible books in the Bible. It's the very last book. That makes sense because it tells us all about the end of the world and even about heaven. Revelation is the apostle John's written record of the vision God gave him of the future. We'll see that Satan and everyone who rejects Jesus will be judged at the end of time, but we'll get to live in heaven forever!

Plot Your Course

Part 1: Churches, Take Care! (Revelation 1–3)

To start off Revelation, John saw a vision of Jesus in all His glory and power. This vision was very different from how John remembered Jesus when He was on earth. When He comes again, it will be with a powerful display of glory. Then Jesus told him to write down what He was about to show him about the end times. But first, Jesus had a few words for seven different churches. Jesus gave them each something like a report card to show them the progress they were making.

Part 2: The Future Despair (Revelation 4–18)

The event that will kick-start the end times is the rapture. The rapture is when Jesus will swoop down toward the earth and take His church—every single Christian living on earth at the time—with Him to heaven. No one but God the Father knows when this will happen.

The tribulation will start right after that. This is what most of Revelation talks about. The tribulation is a seven-year period of time. The first half will be pretty mild, but the second half will be the most destructive, violent time in human history—worse than all the earth's wars and disasters combined!

Here are just some of the things that will happen:

- natural disasters like famines, earthquakes, hailstorms, the sun going dark, the moon turning red, and stars falling from the sky
- *un*natural disasters, like wars, scorpion-grasshopper hybrids stinging people, and fallen angels going around killing people

In the end, a huge number of people will die.

Why is the tribulation going to happen? God has waited thousands of years to give people a chance to stop sinning against Him and follow Him. One day, He'll finally decide enough is enough. Then He'll pour out His judgment and anger on the earth, as He did with the flood in the time of Noah.

Even though Christians will be gone before the tribulation starts, the people left on earth will have a chance to believe in Jesus and follow Him. A total of 144,000 Jews will become believers—and a huge number of non-Jewish people will too!

But Satan will do everything he can to stop the people on earth from being saved. He'll give power to a man called the Antichrist. Halfway through the tribulation, the Antichrist will set himself up as "god." And the whole world—besides believers—will fall for it and worship him!

After the one true God sends more judgments and punishments on the earth, Jesus Christ will finally come and put a stop to everything.

The new earth will have a capital city called New Jerusalem. Revelation describes it as a huge cube floating just above the surface of the earth. It's going to look like see-through gold with brilliant, sparkly light. Also, it's possible that we will be able to move up and down in it, not just side to side.

We will have glorified bodies like the one Jesus had after He rose from the dead. His new body could move through doors and walls. He could suddenly appear and disappear. Our new bodies won't get old or sick or die.

Heaven is not going to be some boring place where we all sit on clouds and play harps. God is going to keep blowing our minds with His glory, power, and majesty—forever!

Part 3: The Ultimate Repair (Revelation 19–22)

When Jesus returns, He'll destroy His enemies, including the Antichrist, in the battle of Armageddon. Then He'll put Satan in prison and take His rightful place as King of the earth.

Jesus will reign on earth for 1,000 years. We call this the millennium (a word that means "thousand"). He will fix the earth and make it beautiful again. There will be justice and peace.

At the end of the 1,000 years, God will release Satan from his prison, and Satan will lead an army of people against the Lord. God will defeat them with fire from heaven with just a snap of His fingers, and then Satan will be thrown into hell forever. Every single unbeliever throughout history will also be judged and sent to hell forever.

Then at the very end of time, Jesus will destroy this earth and create a completely new one—as well as a new heaven. This new heaven and earth will be more amazing than anything any of us have ever seen or experienced on this earth. We call this the *eternal state*. There won't be any more pain, crying, or death. And we'll get to live with God Himself forever!

This is all because of the incredible plan God has had since the beginning of time. In the book of Genesis, Adam and Eve sinned against God, so God promised that He would send a Savior to fix what they did. And He did: He sent Jesus, who died on the cross and paid for all of our sins, meaning we can be made right with God again.

In the end times, Jesus will come back to earth, destroy Satan, and reign as the true King forever. This is the whole story of the Bible: God loves you so much that He did everything He could to save you. He wanted to make sure you could be with Him in heaven forever!

EXPECT THE UNEXPECTED

At the end of time, Jesus will make a brand-new heaven and a new earth. "New" means it won't work the same way our current earth does, with light and gravity and all of that. God will be the light. The rest, we'll just have to wait and see! It's going to be wild!

Enjoy Your Trip

Obeying the Book

Did you know there's a special blessing for you if you obey the book of Revelation? John wrote that God "blesses all who listen to its message and obey what it says" (Revelation 1:3). So how do you obey Revelation? It means to make sure you remember what's going to happen one day: Jesus will come back, defeat Satan, and make a new world for us to live in. Thinking about those things will help you live your life in a way that pleases God.

Making It Count

If you've received Jesus Christ as your Lord and Savior, your name is written in His Book of Life. That means you're going to heaven! But in heaven, you're also going to be rewarded for what you did in your life on earth. Look up and read 2 Corinthians 5:10. What are some good things you can do right now that will count for eternity?

Where's the Gospel?

Sin has infected the whole world, but Jesus brought the cure for sin. At the very end of time, Jesus will get rid of all sin and evil forever. But to spend eternity with Him in heaven, you have to choose to follow Him first. If you've already chosen Jesus, you can celebrate what's in your future! But if you haven't chosen Him, you can do so right now.

God loves you so much, and Jesus wants to forgive you of your sins. Then He wants to take you on an adventure beyond your wildest dreams, with heaven as your destination. As we make our landing after soaring through the entire Bible, all you have to do is say yes to Jesus, and you can soar with Him forever!

IS YOUR NAME IN THE BOOK?

Congratulations! You made it through our look at the whole Bible. We're done with *soaring*. Now it's time for *searching* our own hearts. As we come in for a landing, I want to share a few last thoughts with you.

Over the past 2,000 years since Jesus went back to heaven, He has changed the lives of millions of people all around the world. If all their stories were written down, that would fill a lot of books!

But only one book matters in the end. The Bible talks about something called the Lamb's Book of Life (Revelation 13:8). That's where God records the names of everyone who has been saved because they believed in Jesus Christ. I pray that your name is in there. If you're not sure if it is, you can fix that.

All you have to do is place your trust in Jesus. He did all the work to get you into heaven. He died on the cross for your sins. He is willing to forgive you if you let Him. Why not pray this simple prayer? (As you do, mean it from your heart!):

Dear Jesus, I need You. I know that I am a sinner. I believe that You died for me. When You rose from the dead, You made it possible to erase all my sins. Please do that now. Thank You for loving me so much. I love You too. I want You to be my Savior, and I want to follow You as my Lord. Amen.

If you prayed that prayer, you now belong to Jesus. You are part of God's special family! You just made the best decision you can ever make. That's awesome! Now go and tell someone that you just prayed this prayer to ask Jesus into your life.

Here are some tips to help you stay strong as a follower of Jesus: Keep reading your Bible. Find a church that teaches the Bible, and go regularly. Talk to God regularly during the day, and look for ways to serve Him by helping others out. Tell them about Jesus. Tell them what He has done for you and how He can do it for them too.

Following Jesus is the greatest adventure you can have in life. My prayer for you is that you will get to know Him better and better. When you do that, you will trust Him more and more. Your life will gain meaning and purpose (and joy!). You will be able to face hard times and enjoy good ones.

Finally, here is a special blessing God told Moses to share with His people (see Numbers 6:24-26 TLB). I pray it now for you: "May the Lord bless and protect you; may the Lord's face radiate with joy because of you; may he be gracious to you, show you his favor, and give you his peace."

TELL YOUR MOM AND DAD
ABOUT THE GROWN-UP VERSION
OF THIS BOOK!

SKIP HEITZIG

THE BIBLE FROM 30,000 FEET

SOARING THROUGH THE SCRIPTURES
FROM GENESIS TO REVELATION

Learn more at
BibleFrom30kBook.com.

To learn more about Harvest House books and
to read sample chapters, visit our website:

www.harvesthousepublishers.com

HARVEST HOUSE PUBLISHERS
EUGENE, OREGON